Children have Changed

Copyright © 2024 Esther Evans
All rights reserved

ISBN-13:9798325680977

First Edition published by Niven-Taylor Publishers

All rights reserved. No part of this publication may be
reproduced or transmitted in any form or by any means,
electronic, mechanical including photocopying, recording
or any information storage or retrieval system, without
prior permission in writing from the author.

Cover Title 2024 Book Cover Zone

ESTHER EVANS

Anyone in contact with young children
needs to read this book.

Children

have

Changed

SUPPORTING CHILDREN IN A RAPIDLY CHANGING WORLD.

For Ruby, Lydia and Gracie

Contents

Introduction..1

The Current Context.............................6

The After effects of a Pandemic................8

The Importance of Early Intervention............11

Chapter 1. Negative Effects of Screen Time.......15

Chapter 2. Delayed Emotional Regulation.........43

Chapter 3. Resolving Sleep Disturbance..........85

Chapter 4. The Effects of Diet on Learning......107

Chapter 5. Advice on Self-help Skills............131

Chapter 6. Supporting Schematic Behaviours....153

Chapter 7. Supporting Delayed Motor Skills......179

Chapter 8. How to Support Sensory Behaviours..193

Chapter 9. Delayed Speech, Language and
Communication Skills............................213.

Conclusion.......................................237

vi

Introduction

Children have Changed

Children have Changed

Introduction.

This book is for anyone wanting to give young children all the key ingredients they need to thrive.

Maybe you are wondering why parenting seems so *hard* these days. Perhaps you are a teacher, wondering why teaching has become so difficult and you are worried about the changes you are seeing in your children's behaviour recently. You might feel under pressure for your children to reach targets or milestones that seem impossible when children seem to have a completely different skill set to a few short years ago? You are not alone in this.

Maybe you work in the education system (like me) and are finding it a challenge to deal with the increasing numbers of children being referred in for additional support. There are pressures everywhere, but the funding can only stretch so far and it's *so* frustrating; especially when we all want the same thing. We're all trying to make sure children to have the best start in life, the gold standard life chances to learn and thrive.

I'm guessing that's why you picked up this book.

Children have Changed

I want that too. That's what led me here. I wrote this book to help you understand the reasons behind the sudden, startling changes we are seeing in children. I want you to have the knowledge, understanding and tools to help children feel happier, healthier, less anxious and ready to learn, so they can soak up new skills like a sponge.

I've been a school advisor for many years and I've always enjoyed training and guiding early years practitioners, but recently, many of us seem tired and overwhelmed by the changes in children. Childcare settings and schools are struggling to recruit good staff. Headteachers and childcare managers are feeling jaded, trying to manage yet more demanding, complex children with less money. They are angry and they have every right to be.

Based on our current measures, large numbers of children are entering school with significantly delayed skills. They have extremely limited attention, poor focus, little or no speech, often are still in nappies and they come with a range of unwanted and often aggressive behaviours. The result is beginning to look like organized chaos. What once worked, no longer works. Children have changed.

Children have Changed

In my own home city, the birth rate is actually falling, yet the number of children presenting with delayed skills continues to sharply increase. If we keep going at this rate, soon we will have more children in specialist placements than in mainstream education. Surely this can't be right!

After another exhausting day, I sat in my car with my head in my hands and wondered how on earth we could turn the tide. That's when I started investigating all the reasons why our children could be so delayed and researching all the positive ways we can support them. That research steadily grew and morphed into this book... an explanation of why children's behaviour has changed and more importantly, what we can do about it.

This book is intended for anyone working with, or living with young children. If you do fall into that category, like me, we're in such a privileged position. The way we support children today will determine their future life chances.

The advice and strategies I've included are practical, inexpensive and can help you immediately. I've signposted you to other great places for further support wherever I can. In my career I've been fortunate to work with some amazing and inspirational practitioners who I am indebted to, and I'd love to pay some of that forward.

Children have Changed

The case studies are true, but I've obviously changed names, and identifying factors to preserve the privacy of the families I work with. The subtitle of each chapter are actual comments that teachers have made to me over the past few years. I'll explain why children are behaving in certain ways and how we can quickly and effectively adapt to meet children where they are. The book is my opinion and of course, is open to challenge, but I've aimed to be as truthful as possible and tried to include and share as much knowledge as I possibly can with you.

I hope it will help you understand how children are trying their best to communicate with us through their behaviour and I hope it gives you the confidence and the knowledge to support them, as they grow up in a rapidly changing digital world. It will also hopefully reassure you that there isn't necessarily an epidemic of autism or ADHD. Many children have had a tough time over the past few years and early traumatic experiences can sometimes present with identical symptoms to neurological conditions. We need to stay curious if we are going to work out what's really going on and avoid diagnosing children before we've fully explored possible environmental factors.

Children are changing and that means we have to change too. It's the only way, if we are going to give them the skills to navigate their future. With so much uncertainty in the world, we need to keep this high on the agenda. Right now, too many of our youngest children are anxious, frustrated, angry and fearful. Fast

Children have Changed

forward to their coming of age over the next few decades and society will look a very different and quite frankly, scary place, unless we start to meet these children where they are now.

There is a staggering statistic from the UK office for National Statistics that none of us are talking about. Children born in the UK today have a shorter life expectancy than their own parents. On average 5 years lower! For girls, it's a sobering 4.7 years and for boys a startling 5.5 years. Yet, this worrying statistic barely made the headlines.

From the beginning of time, humans have outlived their ancestors. We've evolved to grow stronger and taller. We've designed ground-breaking medicines and vaccines, we understand diet, nutrition, exercise and the importance of hygiene better than ever before. We've developed science that enables us to reach planets and see galaxies beyond our imagination and we have more information at our fingertips or voice control than ever before. More information is available than we will ever have time to read, process or need. Longer life should be easier than ever to achieve. What on earth is going wrong?

Children have Changed

The current context.

In schools and homes up and down the UK, those raising and educating children are saying the same thing. *Children have changed.* They have more complex profiles; worryingly fewer skills and they know far fewer words and language patterns. In practice, more children are emotionally distressed and take longer to settle when they start school as they can't communicate their needs to the adults. Many are still in nappies, long after they need to be, and there is a swell in childhood patterns of disrupted sleep and limited diets.

Teachers are struggling to deal with children who can't follow a routine without intensive adult support and who display behaviours more akin to babies and toddlers. Behaviours like tipping up toys, throwing objects, climbing the furniture and wandering off with little awareness of their own safety. Children's attention spans are extremely limited and their anxiety is heightened. Many haven't even developed pretend or imaginative play skills yet. Teachers are facing a new frontier.

Recently, I've witnessed an unprecedented amount of delay in all areas of child development:

Communication and Interaction skills
Physical skills
Cognitive skills

Children have Changed

Self-help skills
Emotional and Social skills
… are all rapidly declining.

After the pandemic, referrals asking for early childhood support and interventions have more than doubled. My colleagues regionally and nationally are all experiencing similar rises with statistics beginning to emerge to prove it and Early Years education is a now a major area of concern and priority in many local authorities. This is partly a result of the pandemic restrictions but it's also because of the changes in society that the pandemic brought about.

Children have Changed

The After-Effects of a Pandemic.

What is going on out there? When we opened our doors again after lockdown, we could be forgiven for thinking we were in a science fiction movie and alien children had replaced our human ones. Our children may not look different, but something quite fundamental and profound is happening. Their brain chemistry is literally changing… changing at an alarming rate… and not for the better. I'll explain more about this later.

Parents, childcare practitioners and teachers are struggling with this, and our children are struggling too. They are floundering in a system designed for a different, "previous" kind of child.

Of course, there are also children who escaped relatively unscathed by the last few years of lockdowns, social isolation and mask wearing, but those children are entering the same classes as children who've been adversely affected. And as the saying goes, A rising tide carries all ships.

The growing number of children falling to meet their expected milestones is impacting on every child. These children, through no fault of their own, take up more adult time, more energy and more stamina. In blunt terms they cost the system more, meaning less attention for everyone else. Also consider that fewer typically developing children in each class means

Children have Changed

there are fewer role models in each class and as it's reckoned children learn 80% of everything from other children, that's not good news.

As Bill Gates once said:

"The first five years have so much to do with how the next 80 turn out."

The effects of the pandemic haven't just gone away. We all experienced a collective trauma, a kind of national anguish, particularly around the time the death count was rising daily. None of us need reminding how we were subjected to depressing news bulletins, locked in our own homes, separated from our friends and extended families. It's a very British trait to *Keep Calm and Carry On*, but in many respects, it's as though it never happened.

Extra funding, originally allocated to mitigate the effects of the pandemic has severely and suddenly reduced. School inspectors are back, grading schools again. It's business as usual. Crack on, folks. It might all seem like a distant nightmare, but the pandemic did happen and for our young children it has definitely impacted them. Our current four-year-old children have spent almost a quarter of their young lives in pandemic conditions.

Only now, the true legacy of lockdowns, social distancing, mask wearing and shutdown of core

Children have Changed

services is coming to light. The scale of children suffering from anxiety, even in the early years, is frightening. According to NHS England data, 20.3% of eight-to-sixteen-year-olds already had a probable mental health disorder in 2023.

(Source -The Mental Health of Children and Young People in England 2023 Report).

That's approximately six in every UK classroom of thirty pupils. This steep rise in mental health conditions may be due in part to a positive change in our culture as we all now have more understanding of the importance of good mental health, but the truth is, many of our children simply haven't got good mental health. And that includes infants too.

Consider for a moment what it must have felt like to be born into a world where the adults were nervous, anxious and uncertain that we even had a future. Imagine your first impression of the world is one where you're unable to receive hugs from extended families, or see and read people's expressions because their faces are half covered by masks. What must those early experiences have been like for young children? We don't yet know the full extent of the impact the pandemic had on those born into it, we can only try our best to provide the things they missed out on.

Children have Changed

The Importance of Early Intervention.

I'm going to be upfront - I don't have a magic wand. No one does. Anyone who claims they have a quick solution to a societal problem is probably trying to sell you something (or get your vote). What I do have is over thirty years of experience, working in a variety of educational roles, all of them with young children. I work directly with children, childcare practitioners and teachers, every day, to try and change this troubling shift.

Every time I visit a childcare setting or a school the decline in children's attention and listening skills and the increase in aggression is glaringly obvious. Sometimes, the adults have a pleading look in their eye, hoping I'm going to say:

Here, let me remove all those wild children for you so you can start to teach again.

Of course, the solution is never going to be that easy. The huge increase in the number of children experiencing delay, means we are quickly running out of specialist placements and will necessarily have to cope with significantly delayed children in our mainstream schools over the next few years. If this all sounds bleak and hopeless, please don't despair! You are here, reading this, and that means you *care*. Caring

Children have Changed

adults are the only way to undo the damage of the past few years.

We can't blame the pandemic alone. Even before COVID 19 arrived in March 2020, children's speech, language and communication skills were in rapid decline, UK childhood obesity rates were embarrassingly high, and childhood screen time was increasing to the detriment of physical play and old fashioned, underrated fresh air. When the pandemic came along, it exacerbated all of those already rumbling problems and rolled them into a huge ball. A ball that is still rolling, gathering speed and freight on a daily basis.

This is a tough time to be a child but there is plenty to be hopeful about. The world is full of adults who are passionate about supporting young children to overcome their anxieties and to help them feel a deep sense of wellbeing; undoubtedly the key to unlock learning. The earlier we provide children with the right support, the more hope they have of developing into well-rounded, successful, happy adults.

It's also a tough time to be a parent. Parent mental health is an area that has rapidly declined over the past few years. Many of the parents that I work with openly admit their mental health struggles and that can only be a positive thing. Mental health needs to be talked about because anxiety and depression doesn't just affect adults. There is always a knock-on effect on the

Children have Changed

children. We need to acknowledge this so that we can help.

If you too have noticed changes happening; if you are struggling to cope with children who seem unable to listen or give their attention; if you've noticed children are downright different, stick with me and read on. In the following chapters you will find sensible advice and the tools to begin to change children's futures for the better. In the first five years of a child's life, we can have more impact on their developing brain chemistry than at any other time in their life. But we need to act now, because you only get one chance at childhood.

Children have Changed

Chapter 1

The Negative Effects of Screen Time.

Can Anyone Help Me Surgically Remove an iPad?

Children have Changed

Children have Changed

Case study: Warwick.

*W*arwick, a three-year-old little boy, new to the area, needed to be assessed before he started Nursery school. The referral I received from his health visitor was a bit sketchy. It mentioned Warwick had some developmental delay, but there were no health reports or medical notes, and mysteriously, not even an address on his form. At least there was a phone number so I phoned Warwick's mum, Katie, to ask if I could do a home visit to meet Warwick.*

"We're living in a refuge, sorry love. I can't disclose the address." Katie spoke with a distinctive Scottish accent.

"No problem. We'll find somewhere else to meet. Can you tell me a little about Warwick."

"He's definitely on the spectrum. Autistic, y'know love? He only eats beige food and he needs his iPad on all the time. Right through the night. He keeps us all up at night with it."

"You have other children?

"Aye, another seven, love. They've all got autism."

Keen to know more, I "borrowed" a classroom in a Nursery school and met Warwick after the children

Children have Changed

had gone home, as Katie ominously informed me that Warwick wouldn't tolerate any other children near him. A large boy with dimpled cheeks and a shock of blonde hair, arrived in his pushchair. He held an iPad so close to his face I had to peer behind it to see him properly.

"Shall we get you out of the pram?" I asked.

"Oh, he won't get out, love," Katie said.

"Can you take the iPad away for a minute so I can talk to him?"

"He won't like it, love. I wouldn't."

"Let's at least give it a try. I can't assess him if he's distracted by a screen."

Katie looked on nervously as I edged the iPad out of Warwick's hands. A wail as loud as an air raid siren filled the empty classroom. Warwick threw himself back in his pushchair, bucking his body, contorting himself into a full gymnastic crab position, his head banged the side of his pushchair. His feet kicked out at me. The wailing went up a few decibels.

"Shall we get him out of his pram?" I ventured, but it was impossible for Katie to hear me above the noise.

I'd set out a lovely selection of sensory toys, ready for Warwick to play with, but he was having none of

Children have Changed

it. He screamed until his face went blue. He gagged. He sobbed. He raged with unimaginable fury.

"Does this always happen when you take the iPad away?"

"Och aye, love. You can't take it off him." Katie shrugged nonchalantly, despite the infant inferno erupting between us.

A teacher put her head around the door, curious at the cause of such angry wailing. Warwick's forehead was damp with the effort he was exerting, his cheeks were wet from crying. Blotchy red spots appeared under his pale skin. His eyes looked glazed, hungry, hollow.

"Everything ok in here?"

I nodded sheepishly. Katie looked to me for approval, before she put the iPad back in her son's desperate, snatching hands. That's when I really took notice. It was chilling. Warwick's distress was soothed instantaneously. It was unnatural. His high-pitched cry stopped mid wail. His gaze fixated on the screen. His chubby hands grabbed greedily at the screen. It took less than a second for him to calm down. He'd had his fix. He was soothed. But at what cost?

Warwick was a child that had been through a considerable trauma. During the first lockdown, his parents had split up but neither could leave the house

Children have Changed

and things soon escalated into domestic violence. As soon as society started to open up again, Katie moved the family several times, finally ending up in a women's refuge. Throughout this time, Warwick had learned to use a screen as a soother to the extent he could no longer self soothe.

(More about Warwick later).

Is screen time really that bad?

Please don't think I'm against screens. I'm not. In fact, as my eldest daughter and granddaughter live in Dubai and my middle daughter lives in New Zealand, I couldn't live without them. Technology brings us together when we can't be there in person, it provides education, information, entertainment, reassurance and comfort. You could take many things off me, but I will go kicking and screaming to my grave before you take away my family WhatsApp group or my TV dramas after a hard day's work!

In every nation of the UK, Information Technology (I.T.) is part of the school skills curriculum. We are actively encouraged to introduce children to IT skills from an early age as it will supposedly enhance their everyday lives. There is a lot of common sense behind this. Children are growing up in world where technology prevails. We have a duty to prepare them for that world. We don't know for sure what kind of jobs will even exist when today's nursery children enter the workforce, but I'd risk my house to bet

Children have Changed

screens will be a part of almost all their future work lives. The trouble is, a growing swell of evidence predicts this will also have a significant cost on their emotional wellbeing.

My definition of screen time for the purpose of this book, is any screen that emits a blue light.

- o computers
- o tablets
- o laptops
- o iPads,
- o Kindles or other reading devices
- o TV screens
- o smartphones.

In fact, pretty much every screen you can think of.

Blue light addiction

Recently, I've seen a worrying upward trend in the number of young children, like Warwick, who can't soothe themselves without a screen. Children who become inconsolable. Cuddles or kisses from their parent, softly sung nursery rhymes, bright, interesting toys, beautiful books, all fail to comfort them. Nothing seems to work. But pass them a screen and it's like a magic bullet. The child becomes fixated and instantly stops crying. Now, I'm no addiction counsellor, but what does this look like to you?

It's no coincidence that the largest, most intelligent brains in the world are working away in Silicon Valley to keep us hooked to our smart phones with sneaky

Children have Changed

strategies like faves and likes. In addition to those hooks, that keep us coming back for more, the blue light behind your screen is highly addictive. (If you are reading this electronically, please stick with me anyway). Blue light has been proven to light up the same receptors in your brain as a Class A drug, Heroine and Crack cocaine being in that same category.

Blue light can disrupt our natural sleep patterns. Too much screen exposure can interfere with the bodies' natural circadian rhythm and mess with our melatonin, the hormone responsible for good quality sleep. It can overstimulate us, a bit like having huge amounts of caffeine, so we end up prioritising screen time over going to bed and getting a decent night's rest. It can lead to reduced motivation and addiction-like behaviours in both children and adults. That's before we even think about related eye strain and long periods sitting, without physical movement.

Like most pleasures in life, screen time is fine in small doses. But when it becomes compulsive and the negative impacts outweigh the positives, like in the case of Warwick, we need to act.

Considerations for pandemic babies.

Let's all collectively agree that working from home whilst trying to educate our own children was not easy! Trying to pretend you were the consummate professional on a Zoom call or Teams meeting when

Children have Changed

you had a toddler pulling at your ankles, smearing buttered toast up your legs or moaning about their full nappy was both unrealistic and very stressful!

How many parents had to cope with their child acting up, just as a full contingent of work colleagues entered their living room or bedroom? It's no wonder we all got a bit slack with the screen time we allowed our children to watch during lockdowns. TV stepped in as the babysitter when we needed to work. It was a godsend. Children, placid in the reflected glow of addictive blue light, meant we could still work and pay the bills.

Social media platforms became essential when we couldn't see our extended families and friends face to face. We did whatever we had to do to get through those times and got through them we certainly did. But with hindsight, we can reflect and learn from the research carried out during those dark days.

A study of the nature and pattern of screen time was carried out in the first 15 weeks of lockdown in the UK, led by Dr Nayeil Gonzalez-Gomez of Oxford University. She looked at screen use pre and peri lockdown and has since followed this study up to the present day, examining patterns of behaviour in young children.

During the first lockdown in 2020, the results are phenomenal. The amount of time babies spent watching TV more than doubled. Virtual interactions

Children have Changed

as opposed to face-to-face interactions more than tripled. Virtual interactions with other children, as opposed to face-to-face interactions also tripled. Children's screen time went off the scale.

We are talking here about children who are now entering our Nursery and Reception classes. During the pandemic, these children had a significantly altered experience to all other children that came before them in previous years. Pandemic babies and toddlers were exposed, beyond a shadow of a doubt, to massive increases in screen time. Think back for a moment to spring 2020 when the sun shone, roads were empty, parks deserted.

Today's young children have spent a large percentage of their life in pandemic conditions. We need to keep talking about this because when we plan for these children, we have to take it into consideration. These children have different starting points and different skills. Swiping left and right and tapping icons to find a favourite program is now built into every child's automatic response system. The downside is, many children have far too many gaps in other areas of learning.

Even before the pandemic struck, we knew that children were already spending more time on screens and less time outdoors than in the past. Back in 2006, Sue Palmer in her book Toxic Childhood, identified many of the concerns technology was already imposing on our young children's lives. The pandemic

Children have Changed

isn't completely responsible, but it's certainly speeded things up. If we were on the screen time hamster wheel before, we're now spinning full pelt and the brakes have come off.

The post-natal technology trap.

With the explosion in digital technology over the past twenty years (Google began in 2004, followed by You Tube in 2005), there has been another, more sinister bi-product. A boom in products aimed at young parents, that include screens aimed at babies. Screens are infiltrating places where screens would previously have been unheard of. Retailers are targeting our children from the day they are born and by association, inadvertently touting a blue light addiction.

Did you know you can now buy a baby changing mat that has an inbuilt clear window for an iPad or tablet so your baby can be distracted by a screen as you change their nappy? Many cars are now designed with screens inbuilt into the seats to keep children amused from the moment they leave the maternity ward, and for babies who want to use the remote control like their parents, there are replica remote control toys so they can start to practice from the moment they can hold an object.

In the UK, a growing number of children acquire their first smart phones as toddlers.

Children have Changed

Ofcom's latest report states that:

- 17% of three to four year olds have access to smart phones.

- 24% of five to seven year olds now own their own smart phones.

- 76% of five to seven year olds use a tablet.

- 32% of parents of parents of five to seven year olds report that their child uses social media independently.

- By age 17, 100% of adolescents have access to a mobile phone.

In the last few years there has been a surge in TV programs produced for and aimed at babies and toddlers. YouTube is awash with clips aimed at the baby market. Before babies are even able to focus on their parent's face or follow a moving object with their eyes (around three months), or see the full spectrum of colours (four months), they are vulnerable to a world that seems to approve of pushing screens on babies.

Even baby monitors now have screens attached, so if your baby wakes, you can see and talk to them from another room, taking us a step further from face to face, skin to skin comfort. Baby and toddler toys include an array of pretend screen monitors so even if they aren't in the 17% of toddlers already in

Children have Changed

possession of a smart phone, they can role play having a screen in preparation for when they do get one.

The National Institute for Health and Care Excellence (NICE Guidelines) suggest that young children should have screen free days every week, but, in any case, a maximum of two hours screen time a day is the current guidance. The American Academy of Paediatrics recommends that digital media should be avoided altogether for children under eighteen months, (except for occasional digital chatting to extended family), due to the related links to early language delay.

How many children are exceeding this, not by a few minutes, or even a few hours, but dangerously, perilously over the limit?

When screen time becomes toxic.

Last year, an American study was published that looked at the correlation between the age you receive your first smartphone, and the likelihood of mental illness. The results prove a quite horrifying negative effect on both sexes, but it's particularly startling for girls. Jonathan Haiat's research found:

- o the likelihood of having suicidal thoughts or intentions

- o a sense of being detached from reality

- o aggression towards others

Children have Changed

○   a predilection to addictions and hallucinations

…. all increase, the younger you get your first Smartphone. The study only starts at five years but as we've already seen, according to OFCOM, approximately 17% of toddlers in the UK already have access to a smartphone by then and I've certainly come across children younger than two who know exactly what to do when handed a smartphone.

Twenty years ago, we worried that having the TV on constantly in the background was distracting to a child's developing language skills. Today's parents face significantly more challenges in protecting their child from the insidious effects of a digital world?

Richard Carr warned us how the internet is actually changing the physiology of our brains in his ground-breaking book The Shallows. The title of the book is a brilliant but ominous warning. The internet, originally hailed as a way of improving human intelligence is actually having the opposite effect.

Scrolling through a medium where distracting pop-ups blindside us at every click and a never-ending choice of popular culture stories lead us down rabbit holes means we are actually altering our brain physiology. We are moving down a path toward splintered attention, difficulty concentrating, and an altogether shallower experience of learning.

Children have Changed

I count myself in this category too. I'm often snared into clicking on a celebrity photo headline to see how different an actress looks today, only to be lured into clicking pages and pages of adverts. And why am I even looking for the surprising truth about celebrity couples who've split when I only turned my laptop on to check my emails? Darn it! We all do it. We are all doing less in-depth learning and more skimming and skipping. If you are working with young children, does this ring any bells with you? Are your children's concentration and attention skills improving from additional screen time? In my experience it's the complete opposite, every time.

Controlling content.

Next time your child is watching a screen take five minutes to listen in.

- o Do you hear the kind of language you want to encourage for your child?

- o Is there any violence going on?

- o Even if the images aren't violent what kind of language is used?

- o Is there bad language, for example in the lyrics or in the story?

- o What are the values, hopes and dreams of the characters?

Children have Changed

o   How are women and girls portrayed?

o   How are men portrayed?

o   What are the adverts pushing?

Basically, does the content portray the kind of values you want for your child? Think carefully about this because as adults, we have the ability to read between the lines, to "get" the humour and to make inferences that young children aren't at a stage to be able to do, so try to watch and listen to programmes through their eyes and ears too.

News bulletins are often part of our daily routine, on the hour, every hour, and regarded by most as harmless enough, but although the news may be factual and indeed accurate, we should always remember that it is presented to us through the lens of entertainment and unfortunately, the worst traumas make the best entertainment.

Frequently, we see and hear regurgitated stories of the most horrific events in the world. Events that are totally out of our control. Events that our children are also looking at and listening to. It's worth bearing in mind if we want our youngest children to be less anxious, less depressed and feel more empowered and positive, that we can turn it off. If we need to, we can listen to news on the radio (far less intrusive and

Children have Changed

distressing than seeing images) or catch up later when they've gone to bed.

I love the end of the Richard Curtis film Love Actually when scenes at the arrival terminal are narrated by the Prime minister (played by Hugh Grant).

'Whenever I get gloomy with the state of the world, I think about the arrivals gate at Heathrow Airport. General opinion's starting to make out that we live in a world of hatred and greed, but I don't see that. It seems to me that love is everywhere.'

There are always more positive things happening in the world at any one time, than negatives. The positives just don't get reported on or make exciting headlines. Using the off switch is the key to becoming more connected to the world and finding them.

Case Study: Tenzin's story

I first met Tenzin when he had just started in a busy Nursery school. He was darting about the room, happily enough, so I sat down next to his mum, Panna, to talk to her about her concerns around her son's speech and behaviour.

Tenzin was a precious and longed for child. After ten years of failed pregnancies and many miscarriages, he'd finally arrived and was the subject of plenty of love and attention. Yet at almost three years old, his

Children have Changed

mum was worried that he wasn't saying any words yet. I shared her concerns.

As we chatted, I found out that Tenzin lived in a home where English and Tamil (native language of Sri Lanka) were both spoken. We always allow children with English as an additional language a little longer before we expect to hear them use English words, but Tenzin wasn't saying anything in his first language, Tamil either.

"What does Tenzin like to do at home?" I asked.

"Oh, he loves the iPad. It's his favourite," said Panna.

"Ok," I said (desperately trying not to roll my eyes). "What does he like to watch?

"He likes the wheels on the bus, on YouTube."

"Lovely. And how long does he watch the iPad for?"

"All day long... I can't get it off him. He has it at meal times, in the car, on the sofa... even in the bath."

"Hmmm. Do you ever sing the wheels on the bus to him yourself?"

"No. Only on the iPad, because he loves so much to watch the cartoon bus."

Children have Changed

"Ok," I said, feeling my face colour slightly, "You need to put that iPad in the cupboard and let Tenzin see you sing. He needs to see your face. He needs to watch the muscles in your face move to form words. That song on the iPad is attractive, colourful, and bright. But there is no face for Tenzin to watch. You don't learn to talk from a cartoon bus. It's simply not the same. You learn to talk by watching your parents. Put the iPad away and you sing to your little boy instead."

"In the cupboard?"

"Most definitely!"

"OK. Yes, I can see that. I will try."

Panna was a lovely, kind, well intentioned parent. She'd been distracted, sidetracked, blinded by the flashy but shallow bright lights of the technology trap, just like thousands of other parents. She was true to her word and when I visited Tenzin again, a few months later, he was using many more single words and even a few English phrases. Although still delayed for his age, he was catching up fast. Panna said it was tough at first. Tenzin played up when he couldn't have his iPad, but after a few weeks, his behaviour settled down and as an added bonus, he was sleeping for longer at night.

Children have Changed

Use of Technology in schools

Recently, when I've visited schools, I've noticed songs and rhymes are increasingly delivered through cartoons on an electronic whiteboard. Sometimes, the songs are American versions which may account for the increasing number of children we hear pronouncing words with American accents or using Americanisms like elevator or trash. I always advise the practitioners to turn off the screen. Young children need to see real adults singing songs and rhymes for the following reasons:

- o Children need to see the articulation of the mouth, the shapes it makes as it forms words (lip reading, if you like) when they are learning to talk.

- o They need to hear syllables and see the way our mouths pronounce them.

- o Adults need to role model singing with eye contact and smiles to encourage children to join in.

You can't get this level of interaction from a screen. You just can't. We should be creating a sense of belonging to a group. Early experiences of producing words, sounds and actions have an added power when we are all singing together.

Children have Changed

There are hundreds of nursery rhyme cartoons available and many of these are genuinely lovely. They have bright pictures and twinkly music to accompany the words, they are colourful and child friendly. But, if we are using a cartoon to learn the rhyme The Wheels on the Bus, children may see a red bus trundling along, but they won't see a familiar adult's face, modelling how to make your mouth move so the right sounds come out at the right time, how to articulate words, how to instil a sense of fun, a feeling of belonging. That is what children need first. Then, and only then, we can reinforce it by singing along to cartoons.

The antidote to screen time.

We have to be realistic. We can't eliminate screens. (You won't get mine off me). They are a daily part of all our twenty first century lives in the same way that weather is. There is no point in laying guilt on parents and early years practitioners. Instead, we need information, facts, statistics and advice on alternative ways of using technology to enhance our lives, rather than rule them.

For me, outdoor time is undoubtedly the best antidote to screen time. When we are outdoors, there are certain cells in our eyes that react differently to the light. (I'm no scientist, but I'm told they are called our P-Cells). This works for all genders, but is particularly significant for boys. Natural light soothes our heads, calms us. Daylight is proven to make us feel energized,

Children have Changed

less stressed, and it can soothe and protect us against blue light addiction. Just twenty minutes of daylight can reset our serotonin levels. Imagine that! An antidote that rises in the sky every morning and costs absolutely nothing. Taking children outside daily, if possible, to green spaces is the number one way to mitigate the effects of screen time.

Parent power

The other most powerful tool we have in our toolkit to help children learn about the damaging effects of too much screen time is ourselves. Our intrinsic power as role models means we can teach our children by showing and doing, not just saying and confiscating. But it's harder than we think in a world set up to draw us in. Remember those Silicon Valley techies working against us like a silent, dark insidious force.

It's a sad fact that many parents are also addicted to their phones. I've watched many children at home time, full of anticipation, ready to tell all to their parent about their exciting day, only for their parent to collect them and within seconds turn back to their phone. I've noticed children's faces in this moment. They do everything they can to gain their parent's attention, pulling on arms, whining, repeating phrases like *Look at me Mum!* but sadly, all too quickly, they give up. They trail along behind, body language sagging, faces hurt.

Children have Changed

If we prioritise our phones over our children's desire to communicate with us, their need to share their stories, their hope to have a meaningful relationship with us, we are in danger of raising a generation of restless, emotionless beings with little or no empathy. There it is - that word empathy. The word that any respectable society is built on.

If you want further proof of this, have a look at the clip Still Face Experiment Dr Edward Tronick on YouTube. It's only a short clip, but it demonstrates perfectly the need young children have for our attention and the effect on their emotions when they don't get it.

Warwick.

Warwick (the little boy at the beginning of this chapter) had an extreme screen addiction. He had learned to soothe himself by looking at a screen. It was his comfort, his escape from the noise and chaos surrounding him. His safety blanket. His fix. Removing it was terrifying for him. It may seem cruel to take Warwick's screen away from him. After all, it helped him feel soothed and it stopped him crying, but the same could be said for alcohol, gambling, nicotine or any other hard drug. They all soothe an unmet need at first, but without doubt lead on to bigger health and wellbeing issues later.

Warwick's addiction was so severe, he wasn't yet able to tune into adults to learn new language patterns.

Children have Changed

He'd stopped trying to communicate. He'd withdrawn from the world into his iPad. A familiar world, playing on repeat, gave him a secure, if empty feeling. He wasn't taking part in any other activities and as a consequence, he had considerable developmental delay in all areas. Removing the screen was very painful for Warwick at first. The equivalent of an addict going cold turkey.

The screen time needed to be replaced with adults who soothed and understood what he was going through. He was rocked, sung to and held like a baby. Katie had to persevere through some quite horrendous sleepless nights, but to her credit, she stuck with it. Luckily, Warwick still has a young, adaptable brain and nine months later he is starting to talk and beginning to play. He is a very different child. The neuro-development team assessed him and there is no evidence of him having autism. (Early traumatic experiences can often present in a very similar way to the signs of Autism).

The power of patient, kind and understanding adults always astounds me.

Tips for parents.

- o Rather than use an iPad for stories at bedtime, gradually work towards reading your child a story from a real book or simply talk to your child about their day, recapping their favourite

Children have Changed

part of it, what they had for lunch, what they'd like to do tomorrow, what the weather was like at playtime, or who they played with today.

o Limit screen use - It sounds obvious but setting boundaries is key. Timetable screen time, if it helps. The silence can feel very strange at first, but only in that silence can your child's imagination start to work properly and their dreams flourish.

o Remove phones and turn off the TV at mealtimes. Remember you are your child's number one role model and always will be. What you do, they will do. That goes for swearing, shouting, watching too much TV, smoking and eating a bad diet. You have all the power here. Use it wisely.

o Get outside - make sure every single day has a balance of indoor and outdoor time. Even thirty minutes outdoors can make a huge difference to our mental health and wellbeing.

o If you do use a screen, look into using an app to filter the blue light. Think about installing f.lux on your computer. This software reduces blue light so your eyes stay more relaxed when using a screen. Other options are Night Light on Windows, **Night Shift** on macOS/iOS and Night Mode on Android. You can easily

Children have Changed

google the instructions to do this on almost any device.

- Try not to get to the point where your child is addicted to screens, but if you think they are, talk to your health visitor or GP and your child's childcare or education setting. You need a united front on this. It is very difficult to wean an addicted child off screens, just as it's difficult to stop any advanced addiction but it is possible and it is for their own good. Seek help if you need to. It will be worth it in the long run.

- When you do allow screen-time, try to watch together so you can comment on what you are watching together or talk together about it afterwards.

- Make sure there are always times in the day when you give your child your undivided attention without the distraction of your phone.

- Try to avoid any situation where children are mindlessly watching a screen. Sometimes, we use screens to pacify children. They appear to switch off and become completely passive as they gaze at a screen. This is the exact time when their brain and body need quiet time to rest and process their thoughts. If they don't get a complete switch off time in the day, it can disrupt sleep patterns at night.

Children have Changed

Tips for education and childcare settings:

- o Sing songs and rhymes as a group, with no background music and you as the role model. Instead of a screen, use props like pictures or puppets. Use cartoon songs sparingly and only when the children can all sing confidently, but never rely on a screen to do your job. You are infinitely better than any screen.

- o Talk to your children's parents about the dangers of screen time. Parents are busy people and as the saying goes, you only know what you know. Honestly, if I could go back in time and parent my own children again, I'd do loads of things differently. (And they still somehow grew up into good citizens).

- o Have coffee mornings, stay and chat sessions, and share the current research on screen time with your parents. Give them the knowledge they need to make informed choices. We need to talk about this and work together so that we do all we can to mitigate the damaging effects on children's mental health.

- o Use technology in a way that enhances learning, but don't rely on it. For example, use digital cameras to record special moments, use recordable apps to play back a

Children have Changed

child's new word or song. Use Google images to look at amazing places together as a starting point for a real discussion. The possibilities are endless.

o Consider a policy around limiting screen use in school, in light of the current research.

o Try to avoid situations where children are mindlessly watching a screen and appear to have switched off. We all need quiet times of reflection during a day when the brain can process information but if a screen is playing it blocks this process. Too much screen time is one of the key reasons for disruptive sleep patterns.

Children have Changed

Chapter 2

Delayed Emotional Regulation

Not Another Tantrum!

Children have Changed

Children have Changed

Delayed Emotional Development.

At the start of the first lockdown, a wise, experienced teacher looked at me through the lens of our Zoom call. (How radical we thought we were in those first few weeks when we realised we could see each other through our own computers). Through her little square on my computer, she rolled her eyes and said,

"This is massive. There's no quick fix to this. This is going to take years to unpick."

Her words have come back to haunt me many times as we've tried to work out why children's behaviour has changed so much.

I'm talking about children who fly off the handle, flip their lid and explode with rage for something seemingly insignificant. Children who can't settle when their parents drop them off at school, becoming inconsolable, hysterical. Children full of aggression and frustration. Recently, I've dealt with infant children who've smashed windows, kicked over tables, been involved in head-butting incidents, children who lash out and one child even bit off a part of their support worker's toe.

Parents have told me about children who damage the furniture and smash the TV at home. Mealtimes are battlegrounds and bath times a nightmare. Suspensions and exclusions are happening to younger

Children have Changed

and younger children, even as young as three years old in some cases. Even more worrying, in some respects, are children who appear withdrawn, listless, seeming to lack joy or a lust for life and who don't play. But the most chilling phrase I often hear is, "They've got no empathy."

Many of these behaviours would have been largely unheard of in the under-fives, just a few short years ago, but are recently becoming commonplace. Working in Early Years is starting to feel like working in the Wild West.

What is Emotional regulation?

Children with delayed emotional regulation are a difficult group to deal with because their behaviour packs an emotional punch and can impact the childcare and education workforce as much as it does parents. Emotional regulation starts when a child begins to understand that they are a person in their own right. They gradually develop an early sense of self and start to express their feelings. They start to recognise and manage their own emotions. They also begin to understand that other people have emotions. Hopefully, they start to respond appropriately, for example, they will show concern if another child falls over.

Children can start to show love, kindness and empathy from the earliest stages if we show them how, but if you've been in an Early Years setting lately, you

Children have Changed

could be forgiven for thinking something has gone worryingly wrong in society.

We sometimes use the terms challenging behaviour, unwanted behaviour or disruptive behaviour in the Early Years. I use those terms too. There's no judgement here about what we call it, but we do need to recognise that it's the behaviour that is challenging, unwanted or disruptive and not the child. Personally, I prefer the term delayed emotional regulation to any kind of reference to behaviour, because behind every behaviour, there is always an unmet need. The child with challenging behaviour will be a child with an emotion that is not being met. Identifying that unmet need, is the key to unlock the behaviour. Our challenge as adults, is to identify those inhibitors.

Learning how to deal with your emotions is not easy when you are young and it's perfectly normal for children to have tears and tantrums. They're a natural part of everyone's childhood and to a certain extent, we should accept them. That's not to say we should give into a child's every whim. Far from it. But we are witnessing a worrying increase in behaviours that would normally have started to resolve at a much earlier stage.

Toddlers have tantrums; toddlers throw their toys out of the pram, spit their dummy out, kick and strike when they are overtired, overwhelmed or out of sorts. We all accept that two-year old can and do behave like that sometimes, but as children get older those kinds

Children have Changed

of behaviours obviously become less socially acceptable. Not least because older children are larger, have more physical strength and can cause more damage.

Finding the cause of the behaviour.

Before we can resolve the behaviour, we have to find the root cause. We have to step back for a moment and remind ourselves, as the adults in the room, that this child is in need of something. I'm not saying this lightly because this is not always easy. In fact, sometimes this is really hard. Especially when we are talking about being confronted with behaviours like:

- o Inconsolable crying, sobbing or screaming.
- o Lashing out: hitting, kicking, biting, scratching.
- o Being unable to share toys or resources, snatching or fighting.
- o Becoming aggressive if another child so much as enters their space.
- o Being unable to settle in a setting: Holding on for dear life to a parent.

But we are early years practitioners and we can do hard things. We can. I promise. I'll show you how:

Children have Changed

The reasons behind challenging behaviour.

There will never be one straightforward answer why children struggle to regulate their emotions. Every one of us will have had different experiences in our lives that lead us to activate (switch on) and experience our emotions.

There are as many paths to developing our own emotional regulation as there are individuals in the world. The opportunities we are granted in our life, both positive and negative, help us to process and deal with our emotions. Opportunities like having understanding adults around us, who take the time to explain to us why we are feeling angry or sad, are the kind of experiences that lead us to understand and accept our emotions, meaning we develop skills to regulate and calm ourselves.

On the other hand, a lack of those kind of opportunities can mean we struggle to process our emotions and get stuck in a bad place.

Case study: Nelly's story.

When Nelly was four years old, her mummy died in a car crash whilst on her way to collect Nelly from school. This was understandably a devastating and shocking blow to the family and produced very powerful emotions of grief, loss, emptiness, loneliness and worry. But in many ways, Nelly was lucky. She had opportunities to talk about her feelings.

Children have Changed

Although at the time, her dad was hurting too much to share his own pain, Nelly was able to share her grief in school with her key worker, Rita. She often talked to Rita about her Mummy and how she missed her. Rita spent time looking at photographs with Nelly, talking about and remembering the happy times Nelly had shared with her mummy. If ever Nelly felt sad, she had a trusted person who understood that she had those powerful feelings. Rita was always there to give her a smile and a hug. Rita also helped to give Nelly the language for her feelings.

Rita told her that the funny uncomfortable feeling in her tummy was sadness and if Nelly was ever feeling sad, angry or lonely, it is ok to feel like that. Now, Nelly understands what's happening when those feelings arise. Of course, Nelly still has sad times and angry times. Rita often tells Nelly: We are supposed to feel our feelings. That's what feelings are for: To feel. Even if they make us cry. It's ok.

Feelings that can turn toxic.

Without that understanding and recognition of Nelly's feelings and that emotionally available person to listen to her, Nelly's feelings were at risk of going underground. Feelings are slippery entities. They can disappear from the surface and become more sinister. They can start to mutate into other more toxic feelings like anger, rage and frustration and that can lead to aggression and violence. Our feelings can become

Children have Changed

dangerous. If we keep ignoring them, they can eventually lead to a mental health condition.

Children need to be able to recognise how they are feeling if they are going to start to control their emotions. But we can't always expect young children to be able to do this right away. It takes practice and there will almost certainly be slip ups. But learning to process our feelings is vital if our children are going to have any sense of wellbeing.

The beginnings of mental illness.

If our children are regularly falling into a state of anxiety and distress, their mental health will eventually start to suffer. This is already happening far too frequently in young children. Children who seem inconsolable or full of unresolved rage are children at the very beginning of a mental health condition. The seeds are already planted. If we act now, we can stop them being fertilized and growing into conditions and thought patterns that are difficult to reverse.

We already know that half of all mental health conditions are established by age fourteen. This begs the question, why are we not prioritising mental health at the earliest opportunity, to prevent these conditions developing? Why are we not talking more about this? We are witnessing an increase of under-developed emotional regulation in our children. How many of today's young children will go on to develop a mental health condition by the time they are teenagers? What

Children have Changed

will be the far-reaching consequences on us all in society? I don't think it's scaremongering to say we are on a slippery and dangerous slope. Remember:

- o NHS England found that 20.3% of eight-to-16-year olds already had probable mental health disorders in 2023.

(Source -The Mental Health of Children and Young People in England 2023 Report).

What kind of statistics will be looking at when today's infants become teenagers if we don't start to address this now? We know there is already an increase in children who become aggressive when they can't manage to regulate themselves. How many of those children will go on to develop:

- o Addiction
- o Self-harm
- o Depression
- o Anxiety
- o Harm to others
- o Suicide.

I'm no bookmaker but I can take a guess and it's not looking good. Luckily there are things we can do to reverse this.

Making emotional development a priority.

Young children need adult help to regulate their feelings. Focusing on teaching Literacy and Numeracy is pretty pointless if our children are not in a regulated

Children have Changed

state. If a child doesn't feel secure and stable, their brain will literally stop them from learning. Once we enter into a stressed state, our brain reverts back to its primitive mode of fight or flight. When that happens, our stress hormones flood the part of the brain needed to process new information, with chemicals that make it totally inaccessible. The equipment we have in our brain for learning is literally shut off. We need to remember this before we even think about teaching phonics or numeracy. I'm not saying they are not important but:

If you can't regulate your emotions, you can't access learning.

If you ask me, we should pin this message on every classroom wall, put it above the door in neon lights, tattoo it onto foreheads, print it on placards, set it as daily reminders on phones. Email and write it to senior managers, headteachers, politicians, council members and parents.

Each child needs a trusted adult to help them understand and regulate their emotions. Without that support, we can expect behaviour to quickly deteriorate into:

- o Dropping like a dead weight to the floor.
- o Kicking their legs
- o Screaming, shouting and crying inconsolably.
- o Shedding tears, sweaty palms and red faces.
- o Lashing out if you try to offer comfort.

Children have Changed

- Biting, scratching and pinching.
- Throwing objects.
- Holding onto a comforter for dear life.

There is no doubt about it, these children are in pain, but this is obviously not conducive to learning when another twenty-nine children may be waiting for their teacher to return from the battleground and it's just as difficult and tiring for parents.

Recently, I've met both parents and teachers, so worn down by children's overwhelming displays of emotion, they've started to believe the children have a personal vendetta against them. The children are deliberately sabotaging their classrooms in some kind of revenge ploy. Parents are winding up their child before they arrive, unleashing their Tasmanian devil like a swirling tornado on the class, while they furtively slip away, leaving them to deal with it.

Of course, that's not the case. These children are in genuine distress. What they are feeling is true, deep emotional pain. They have unmet needs. But what are those unmet needs that are so important the child is causing chaos? We need to look for potential triggers. We might not know for sure what has caused a child to become distressed, but we can start to rule out the usual emotional suspects:

- Feeling pain,
- Being fearful or afraid
- Feeling misunderstood

Children have Changed

- o Feeling confused or ignored
- o Needing to be heard or understood
- o Feeling uncomfortable: hungry, thirsty, tired, wet, over-stimulated or bored.

Let's be honest, when there is a full-blown tantrum or meltdown happening it's difficult to think about anything else above the heightened decibels. But we have to try. Every child is an individual so there isn't one, clear answer here. There will never be just one simple solution to emotional regulation, but if we turn detective and try to work it out, we will be at least half way to calming the infant sized bomb going off in the corner (and soothing our own headaches).

Considerations for pandemic babies:

It's important to remember that children who were born post pandemic, have had different experiences to the norm. In their earliest, most formative years, through no fault of their own, those children will have missed out on a significant number of social events so we can't reasonably expect them to be in the same place emotionally, as the children who were born before them. Post pandemic children have had a very different experience of society and we need to allow them special dispensation, because we know that it's the experiences and opportunities that we are granted in life that help us develop emotional regulation.

Children have Changed

Pandemic babies have had:

- o Less birthdays, Christmases, Bar Mitzvah's and celebrations with extended family and friends.
- o Less social experience of supermarkets, shops, hairdressers, cafes.
- o Less opportunity to meet other parents and children for example, mother and toddler groups
- o Less play dates.
- o Less incidental social interactions like chatting to neighbours or to parents at the school gate.
- o Less (if any) face to face visits from a health visitor.
- o Less doctor or hospital appointments (most appointments were over the phone and not face to face).
- o Less visits to the dentist.
- o Less childcare (unless a parent was a key-worker).

Even if a child had a parent who was a key worker and so could still go to school or a childcare setting, children who were allowed to attend had less opportunity to absorb their full learning quotient of emotions because all the adults were wearing masks, the environments were stripped back and there were far less children attending to play with.

Children have Changed

Masks

Ah masks! During the pandemic, masks were obviously important. There were sound, scientific reasons for wearing them. I wore one. No doubt, you wore one. I'm not criticising the rationale for wearing them, but they did have huge, unintended consequences. Mask wearing meant babies and children missed many opportunities to watch and experience real people in real life, expressing their emotions. Laughing, smiling, giggling, sighing, people looking tired or excited, bemused or shocked… All of these facial expressions, and the related emotions were hidden behind masks.

Of course we didn't wear masks at home, but it's impossible to count how many fewer facial expressions our children saw, in comparison to the previous pre-pandemic world where no one wore masks. Children need time to catch up on this.

The Reasons Children need to see our faces.

Babies are constantly searching, primarily their parent's face and then the faces of other adults to help make sense of their world. This is how they begin to tune into others and start to understand their self, their emotions and what those emotions mean. But pandemic babies have had far fewer examples of faces to study. If they were lucky enough to have been born into a family with lots of brothers and sisters around, this may have mitigated some of the effects of masks,

Children have Changed

but children who had a harder lockdown, children who spent long periods of time with very anxious or depressed parents, children who were the only child in a household or children who were particularly isolated due to health conditions in the family will have missed out on lots of incidental learning that we previously took for granted.

This is impossible to quantify. There is no way of counting how many face-to-face interactions each of us has, or in fact, how many different facial expressions we need to witness before we fully understand a related emotional response. How many times do babies see a smile before they understand it means we are happy? We simply don't know, but we do know our children have had far less than normal. We know because of the huge increase in delayed emotional and social regulation. It can't be a coincidence.

Case study: Angus' story

Angus was born in the first few months of the pandemic (May 2020). His Mum had three previous children and felt confident to give birth at home to avoid going into a restricted hospital full of Covid 19 patients. Angus was born at night, by firelight in the family living room with just one midwife attending. The midwife wore a mask throughout the birth but other than it was a normal delivery.

Children have Changed

Angus' Dad has kidney disease so the family had quite a hard lockdown. They didn't go to any social events for at least twelve months after Angus was born and felt quite isolated. Angus has two older sisters and a brother, so as he grew into a toddler, he had role models around, but when he eventually started childcare, two and a half years later, although Angus could talk, he chose not to. He kept to himself in Nursery and reacted badly if another child came close to him or attempted to share his toys. It took a while before he would even make eye contact.

His mum worried (quite understandably) that he may have Autism. Other children seemed to make him anxious and he would lash out if they entered his space. At home, when social distancing restrictions were lifted and extended family were finally allowed to visit, Angus ran away and hid, watching his relatives from behind the sofa or the top of the stairs.

Angus is a lovely, intelligent little boy and has no difficulty communicating at home, but he does have social anxiety. This means his emotional and social skills are delayed. It has taken another twelve months, but Angus is now beginning to make friends in school. His speech is clearer and more recently he will talk to both adults and children. He doesn't have Autism, but his family and his teacher notice he does still have some social anxiety when there are birthday parties or larger events. Angus needs time, patience and understanding adults to help him reach his potential in social and emotional development.

Children have Changed

The legacy of lockdowns

The pandemic was a difficult time for young families. Some households like Angus' family were isolated but they muddled through together, other families found the lockdowns claustrophobic and stifling. Separation rates increased. Add to that, bereavements (233,791 people had Covid 19 recorded as the primary cause of death on their death certificate).

Then there was the stress of trying to work from home, plus grief, anger, financial uncertainty, debt and health anxiety at the slightest cough or cold. Domestic violence statistics rose steadily during and after lockdowns (Source: Office for National Statistics England and Wales) and considering that domestic violence is a very under-reported crime, that's probably only the tip of the iceberg.

No-one got away unaffected. Even pre-natal babies who can hear their mother's voice from the six-month pregnancy mark would have been able to hear those daily news bulletins, waiting and wondering what they were in for as they floated dreamily in their confines. Now, I'm not suggesting for a minute that they would have understood government statistics, but anxiety as we know, is a feeling, and if that feeling is not regulated it stays in the body and can turn toxic. How many of our pandemic babies heard language and sounds that led to early experiences of stress or anxiety? We didn't know for sure, during that time,

Children have Changed

that we would find a vaccine, or be able to return to work, or the death count would stop increasing and start to decline. We didn't know our children would emerge healthy and safe. For a time, we all lived in a bleak, uncertain world.

Covid 19 caused a collective trauma. Nationwide, we were all anxious. The outside world, with its masks and two-meter social distancing, it's roped off hospitals and supermarkets, shortages of toilet roll and queues down the street, looked a very alien, different place.

I know! I want to forget all about it as well, but we have to consider that this was our children's very first experience of social and emotional interactions. Their knowledge and understanding of the world around them were a strangely different experience to anything else in modern history.

Emotional and social development doesn't happen by magic. It happens through interactions with others and it's becoming increasingly obvious that many of our children have big, gaping holes here.

Typical Difficult Emotions in the Early years.

As children grow, they have to learn to deal with a lot of emotions, regardless of pandemics. For a child under five here are some of the most common triggers:

Children have Changed

Frustration.

It can be a frustrating time when you are only little and you have to depend on adults to meet all your basic needs, especially if you haven't got the language to explain what you want. Often, big, loud and aggressive behaviours can be triggered by something relatively small and trivial. Perhaps by wanting something as simple as a drink, feeling hungry, thirsty or maybe feeling lonely and craving some company or attention. Not being able to communicate this is a frustrating thing. Especially when you don't have any words yet.

Having to wait.

Learning to wait is a hard thing when you are little. It takes time. We know that children have typically had fewer childcare sessions and fewer social gatherings over the last few years than they would normally. Quite simply, they may not have had as many opportunities where they've had to wait. Realising that they are not the only person in the world, or indeed the most important person in the world, can be a big blow. It can even cause a physically painful feeling. A feeling of rejection, disillusionment with the world, sadness or hurt pride is awful, no matter what your age. Of course, a typical three-year-old can't put all of that into words. It's much easier to demonstrate their distress by crying, kicking their legs and letting rip.

Children have Changed

Having to share.

Similarly, the reduced opportunities for social interactions with other children over the pandemic, means there haven't been as many chances for children to share toys, share food, or even share their own space. Children need time to practice sharing. It doesn't happen by magic. There is no sharing fairy. (How I wish there was!) Children need repetition of the same messages, sometimes many times, before they fully grasp that the world is not all about them and their super ego.

The word "No".

Children can't always have their own way, just as adults can't, but hearing the word No for the first time and processing what it actually means can be truly devastating. Thinking again about the earliest experiences of our Pandemic babies, is it all that surprising that they may not have heard that particular word too many times? They were born into a world where, in all honesty, no-one knew how many of us would get out alive. How many parents slackened the rules? Gave in? Just in case. And really… who could blame them in that situation?

Children have Changed

The physiology of a tantrum.

Emotions create powerful feelings and while children are in the throes of those feelings, they may be feeling completely overwhelmed. It's as though a powerful surge overtakes their brain and their bodily functions. It's upsetting for us when a child has a tantrum but consider that a child may also be feeling pretty frightened as those strong feelings of rage sweep through them.

And if those feelings have never been talked about, recognised or explained before, it's even worse! How disorientating it must be. Crying, screaming, pushing people away or hitting out may be their outward way of coping. Inside, it's the brain's way of actually soothing and relieving those feelings, discharging all that pent up energy, regulating themselves from the frightening surges of emotion they're feeling inside.

Regulating ourselves.

When that amount of pent-up frustration is unleashed, it can be tiring and emotionally draining on us adults too, so it's important to look after yourself. Allow yourself time to get into the head space needed to deal with such strong emotions. Think of it as the emotional equivalent of taking a deep breath before you dive underwater to save someone else. It's only by allowing yourself time to take in enough air that you are in a position to help. If we use up all our own

Children have Changed

emotional air supply, we will burn out, just when we need to be emotionally strong. None of this is easy. It's blinking hard. But we can do hard things. We work in Early Years for God's sake. We can do anything.

It's impossible to get it right every time. All we can do is try our best with the resources we've got available at the time and be realistic. You only know what you know. I've often wished I could go back in time to parent and teach again with the tools I've leaned over many years, but I can't, so my way of compensating is to pass it on to you, so you don't make the same mistakes I did.

The more energy we invest in the area of emotional and social development, the greater the payback will be later and the greater children's capacity for learning. We should never expect children to be in a constant state of bliss and contentment. It's just not going to happen. All children will have stressful moments as they learn to recognise and control their emotions. That's a natural part of life, but the more we support this area, the calmer our classrooms will be, and the more conducive our environments will be to allow everyone to learn.

Adapting to today's children.

Most children have had less social contact, fewer interactions and less sight of what emotions actually

Children have Changed

look like on people's faces. They've had to deal with more anxiety and stress in the ether.

They are going to need more time than usual to catch up with their emotional and social development.

In the same way it takes practice to learn to read, write, or play an instrument, it takes practice to understand and take control of your emotions.

Adult role models

Early Years practitioners and parents...I'm talking to YOU. Having time to yourself, to look after your health and follow your own interests, makes you a more interesting, well-rounded, emotionally available person for others. I know there are pressures. There are hundreds of goddam daily pressures but you are a key role model, an important influencer. You need to build your own reserves. You deserve them and you need them.

Early years practitioners are a modest group of people in my experience. They sometimes forget that they, along with a child's parent, are a child's most powerful role model. There's a saying that imitation is the sincerest form of flattery, so when a child copies you, take it as just that - a gigantic compliment.

To a young child, you are a giant, a god, you are their whole world, a master of the universe. If you work in early years, you are as powerful as today's most hit

Children have Changed

upon influencers. You are responsible for children's lives at the most crucial point in their lives, in terms of their brain development. You can literally shape children's brains for the better. You can change their future. Our children are watching you for the cues to social behaviour, even if you don't realise it. And what's more, children are infinitely more intuitive than we give them credit for.

Whatever we model, they will copy. Children do what you do, say what you say, and act as you act. The downside is, that goes for the negatives as well as the positives. If you shout angrily, your child will shout back. If you swear, expect bad language to come right back at you. If you are calm, positive and encouraging, so too will your child be. It applies to all aspects of life. Children are watching us all the time, looking to us for their social and emotional cues.

Parenting styles

Generally, in life, we tend to follow the parenting styles of our own parents. Have you ever had that moment where you stopped in your tracks because you've just channelled your own parents' exact tone of voice? Perhaps you were saying something like...

This is the very last time I'm going to say it...I'm not going to tell you again.... (I'm shuddering at the thought).

Children have Changed

Luckily, almost all parents and care givers want the best for their children but sometimes, if we have the awareness to realise that our own role model wasn't a particularly helpful one, we can inadvertently go to the opposite extremes. If a parent gave far too much freedom before we were emotionally ready for it, we can have a tendency to over compensate and become too controlling.

If we were brought up in a parenting style that was so strict we weren't ever aloud to make our own choices or think for ourselves, we can inadvertently over compensate the other way and give too much freedom and not provide enough structure or boundaries for our own children.

There's no such thing as a perfect parent. We're all just muddling along, doing our best with the tools we have in our toolkit at the time, but it's always worth considering our own role models, and staying open to change if necessary.

During the pandemic, Dr Nayeli Gonzalez-Gomez of Oxford University researched the implications and lessons from the lockdowns on our children for the present and future. She studied 892 families across the UK, all of whom had children between the ages of eight months to thirty-six months. Although there were some challenges in gathering direct feedback from parents, the results showed that the families who spent more time taking part in enriching activities like cooking, playing and singing together had children

Children have Changed

who achieved higher results in language production and thinking skills.

The more responsive and sensitive parents were to their children and the greater the variety of activities they were taking part in, the better results the child had in their language and cognitive development. In other words, what happens in the home in the first three years matters hugely for children's early development. That's no surprise, but it's good to have actual proof.

Avoid Negativity

It's a startling fact that every single thing that happens to us is stored somewhere in our brains. We might not be able to recall or retrieve every single experience when we want to, but research has proven that each and every one of those experiences is logged somewhere in our brain's amazing storage facility. That's worth bearing in mind when we sigh heavily, get a bit grumpy, lose our temper or lay guilt on a child.

(*You're making so much noise none of the other children can hear a thing*, or *You've made me so tired after you kept me awake all night*). Messages that carry emotional guilt will be stored in our children's emotional and social DNA. That's why it's important, wherever possible, to avoid using negative messages with children. Being in a good place emotionally ourselves can certainly help.

Children have Changed

"I've learned that people will forget what you said, people will forget what you did, but people will never forget how you made them feel." - Dr Maya Angelou

Developing Emotional Independence.

We put a lot of focus and energy into getting young children to be as independent as they can be in school. Independence is fantastic. It means that children can do things for themselves, freeing us up to be more productive, to spend more time on higher reasoning skills. However, we can sometimes forget that to be independent, you have to first learn to be dependent on another person.

You have to first be able to depend on an adult before you feel confident enough to do things independently. And for some children, that might never have been the case. Sadly, not every child has had previous opportunities to form strong attachments with their parent or main care giver, before they start school. For a myriad of reasons, not all parents are in a place to be able to be that dependable and reliable person. (This is not to judge those parents, but it is to try and support that child).

All is not lost. It's never too late. We can be the person that a child learns to depend on. We can make a secure attachment with them. If a child hasn't previously had a consistent person to respond to them when they cried, or became frustrated, or had unmet needs, *we* can be that person. They can depend on us

Children have Changed

because we show up. Every day. Consistently. By being positive, encouraging, not giving in, and being there for them, we can help children learn how to gradually trust and depend on an adult. Once that trust is there, they can tentatively start to branch out for themselves and learn to become independent.

Somewhere in-between this dependence and independence is a place where boundaries get pushed and tested. Children will test our trust. It's a reasonable thing to do when you think about it. They are checking us out to see if we really are trustworthy. Do our credentials hold up or will we give up on them? It's hard. Really hard at times. They will shout, cry, push and shove, but we can do hard things because we know what a huge difference it will make to that child's life.

We also need to be mindful that if a child has tantrums that always lead to the pleasure of them getting their own way, they will quickly learn to use a tantrum as a strategy to get what they want, over and over again. And again! Because it works. Because children are not stupid. Even if they can't talk, they can often still outwit us! Children are smarter than we give them credit for.

How to handle a tantrum.

Be prepared for the next time a tantrum strikes by following this six-step plan:

Children have Changed

1.H.A.L.T.

The best way to handle a tantrum is to avoid it in the first place so if you spot a child getting frustrated, grouchy or aggressive, try to catch them in the early stages before it escalates.

It can help to remember the acronym HALT. (Hungry? Angry? Lonely? Tired?).

As you notice the first signs of a child becoming dysregulated, use it as a quick checklist to rule out any probable causes. (This can work for adults too). Young children won't necessarily have the vocabulary to explain what they need, so we'll need to do some guesswork. Could they be in need of attention or are they over-tired? Perhaps they need changing? Are they physically hurt? Are they too hot or too cold? Are they over or under stimulated? Can you find and meet that need so they feel regulated again? The aim is to calm the situation before the feeling escalates and the child becomes too anxious.

2. Regulate yourself

I'm speaking from experience when I say it's not always possible to get in first and find the cause so if a child is in the throes of a full-blown tantrum, try to remove yourself (at least in your head) and take a bird's eye view of the situation. Even if you don't feel calm, act calm. Pretend! Have a strategy up your sleeve so you can be ready to regulate yourself when

Children have Changed

you need to. Tantrums are designed to upset our nervous system so we need to do this. Here are a few ideas to try:

- o Count to 10 slowly in your head.
- o Put your hands together and push for a count of 10.
- o Say to yourself *I work in Early years. I can do hard things. I am a goddam badass.*
- o Take a long deep breath in for a count of four and repeat out for a count of four.
- o Remind yourself that there is always wine / chocolate in the fridge / biscuits in the tin.

Whatever it takes for you, take those moments so you are calm.

3. Keep everyone safe.

This is the equivalent of tantrum CPR. If you need to, remove the child from danger, or remove others nearby who may be at risk of getting kicked or having items thrown at them. Remove loose objects around them if you need to. If the child is already in a safe place, leave them be.

4. Stay close.

Don't, I repeat don't, leave the scene. Yes… I know you want to, but children need someone with them to

Children have Changed

be able to regulate, so stay close. Don't crowd them, or try to touch them at this stage but stay within sight. Be mindful of eye contact. Try not to stare or let others stare, as this can inflame feelings of anxiety. Calmly and firmly explain that you are here and you will stay close by until they are ready. We can sometimes feel the need to be in control of a situation by telling a child off repeatedly, but I promise you that at this point in the tantrum, it's better to stay calm and wait it out.

5. Recognise their feelings.

When they start to come back down, approach them and empathise as best you can by saying "I can see you're feeling so angry."

If you can, meet the child at the same level of intensity as they are at, by using a similar tone and volume of voice. This is a technique called effect attunement, often used by psychologists and it can work wonders in bringing a child back down to earth. That's because no matter what your words are saying, if your emotional response is as loud as the child's emotional response, you will be subliminally giving them the message:

Oh my gosh yes, you are in pain. I can feel how awful this is for you. I see your pain and I feel it too.

Try it - It can be a game changer.

Children have Changed

6. Give time.

Children need to be in a state of calm before they can process anything. Remember: If you can't regulate your emotions, you can't access learning. Carefully pick your moment to explain why you said "no" to them (if that was the trigger). Remind them in a firm but soft tone of voice, whatever they need to learn from this, for example, "We don't pinch our friends around here, because it hurts them." Children need to know that we are in control, and we are doing things in their best interests to help them learn.

Have appropriate expectations.

Tantrums are common in young children, especially when they haven't got the language to explain how they are feeling. They most commonly happen around two years of age but following the pandemic, we need to adjust our expectations, bearing in mind the limited social experiences children have had over the past few years.

How to prevent challenging behaviours.

There are plenty of ways to prevent challenging behaviour escalating in the first place. My mantra is always that prevention is better than cure so here's a few of the most successful techniques:

Children have Changed

Proximity praise:

You have to be proactive here. Consciously look for a child doing something they should be doing (maybe they are putting their apron on before they paint, or putting all the cars away when it's tidy-up time). Actively praise them, so the other children in earshot can hear you. This is all about rewarding good behaviour with positive attention; something almost all children want and thrive on. Most children will respond to your cues and start to copy the good behaviour, so give them lots of praise as well. Keep repeating this strategy as often as possible to get lots of positive vibes going.

Reward the good / Ignore the bad:

Most children would rather have some attention, even negative attention, than none at all. Sometimes, you can see this when a child throws a toy or tips up a box, but then looks to you in a kind of challenging way. Their face, with a slight half smile, seems to say What are you going to do about it?

That child is silently challenging you to give them your attention. They are craving it. Any attention is better than no attention. And they've learned that making a fuss, a loud noise or a mess is a quicker way of getting you to react to them than if they toe the line. What's more, the reaction to their negative attention is

Children have Changed

giving them the feeling of satisfaction they are craving.

The answer is to catch this child in a place where you can reward appropriate behaviour. Be proactive and look for the smallest opportunity to praise them. Heap the praise on them initially. Let them feel how good it feels to be the centre attention for good behaviour. Keep repeating this as often as possible and notice the positive changes.

Positive labelling.

You've probably heard of labelling theory. In a nutshell, it means that if we are labelled at an early age, we subconsciously become the label that has been attached to us. If you tell me I'm hopeless often enough, there's a high chance I'll start to act hopeless. If you tell me I'm confident, I'm much more likely to act confidently. There is a lot of power in this. We can plant seeds and suggest to children what we want them to be, as long as we are using helpful, positive labels. This is also a great way to boost their self-esteem. If we want to increase children's empathy, we can remind them how kind they are.

Set boundaries.

Young children need boundaries, both at home and in school. We have to teach them what is acceptable and what's not acceptable or we run the risk of all kinds of

Children have Changed

safety mishaps. In my experience, children like boundaries as long as there are opportunities for them to make choices within them.

Once we've washed our hands we can choose our snack.

Once we're wrapped up warm, we can choose where to play outdoors.

How we teach those boundaries is the key to success. As the responsible adult in the room, we have to remain calm and be consistent. Keeping to the same boundaries for everyone and explaining the reasons why they can't do something is important too. If it's the first time that children have butted heads with a boundary, they are going to feel angry, so we need to help them feel supported and contained, without giving in.

Outdoor time.

The benefits of being outdoors (for adults as well as children) is well documented, but for children who struggle to manage their emotions, outdoor time is essential. When we go outdoors, the light is different, more natural, less harsh, more soothing. Green is a colour scientifically known to soothe us. Fractal patterns like the higher, thinner branches of trees or the patterns of veins in leaves are linked to patterns in our own bodies like the patterns our own veins make, and

Children have Changed

the branch-like structures in our lungs. Subconsciously, natural patterns in the environment can soothe, and regulate us.

If a child gets angry and shouts indoors, the sound remains trapped and rebounds off the walls, whereas outdoors, the sound is set free and floats away. It's a far less stressful environment. We should be taking children outside every day, not least so they don't lose their connection to the natural world, but also because it soothes and calms their brain chemicals, allowing for empathy and understanding to develop.

Listen

Modern life is so busy, isn't it? Allow yourself time to just stop and listen to what children are showing us. Even if they have no words, watch their gestures, body language, their preferred areas to be in, preferred people to be close to and their preferred choice of resources. When we know what motivates our children, we are in an infinitely better place to support them. Never feel guilty about this. Reflection time makes us better people, better parents and better practitioners.

Taking the time to implement a person-centred approach like the work on Helen Sanderson's website can work wonders in bringing together settings with families in the best interest of supporting a child.

Children have Changed

Children can learn empathy and kindness from the day they are born if it is modelled to them. If you work with young children, I'm betting you already have a handle on this. Just keep going. You are amazing!

Should I use time out?

Hmm…Time out can be a contentious issue. In my opinion, prevention is always better than cure so it's far better to set up some quiet, cosy spaces in your environment where children can choose to be alone if they're feeling tired or grumpy. That way, they can give themselves time out without any of the negative connotations associated with it.

If you do choose to use time out, please don't ever remove the child from the room completely. If they've got as far as being in a dysregulated state, remember that they will have an underlying unmet need. It could be they want attention. They could be thirsty. They could be over tired or feeling heightened emotions. Sending them away in that state is never the right thing to do. They still need an adult nearby so stay close.

Sometimes I've come across practitioners who still use a Naughty step or Naughty chair. This is pretty outdated practice now. Think for a moment about the negative connotations of the language, considering what we now know about labelling theory. There are much better ways to deal with unwanted behaviours.

Children have Changed

Trauma Informed practice.

If a parent or teacher shouts or reacts angrily when a child does something that oversteps the boundaries, and the child is left alone with those frightening, unprocessed feelings surging through their body, it can lead to a child developing trauma in just the same way that a traumatic event can. The effect on the brain is identical. Children need to know we have them in our sight. Yes - they have done something wrong and yes - they need to know the consequences, but they are still part of the family, part of the class, they are still on our team and they need to know that even though they've messed up this time, we haven't abandoned them. We will give them another chance.

Leaving a child in distress, with no way of regulating their feelings can eventually lead to them developing a disorganised attachment.

If you can't regulate your emotions, you can't access learning.

Going back before we can go forwards.

We know from previous, well documented work carried out in Romanian orphanages that children thrive, only when they are given human attention and love. Even with all the necessary outward resources they need for survival, without adult attention children will sadly not reach their full potential. We humans are designed to interact. Interactions are what make us

Children have Changed

human. Not all interactions are good ones. They can hurt like hell, but we do need them.

Sadly, for a small percentage of children, regardless of pandemics and lockdowns, they don't always get the quota of positive adult interactions in life they deserve to be able to develop their own emotional regulation. The answer here is we have to go back and revisit the stages they have missed in their early development. Calming, regulating activities should be an essential part of every young child's everyday life. Things that parents do naturally without even thinking about it, like:

- o Giving direct eye contact as we sing, talk and make noises.
- o Cuddling.
- o Smiling.
- o Humming.
- o Playful games like Peek a boo.
- o Swaddling and applying gentle pressure.
- o Repeating familiar words and babble sounds.
- o Rocking, swaying, tapping to a gentle beat.
- o Being sung to in a calm and soothing voice.
- o Giggling with a familiar adult.
- o Being held aloft and then pulled into a cuddle.
- o Rough and tumble play
- o Skin to skin contact with a trusted adult e.g. Round and round the garden game.
- o Looking at books together.

Children have Changed

Where a child has missed out on this emotional learning, we need to go back to the beginning of basic child development and put these foundations in. Sometimes, practitioners and teachers can be wary of rocking or holding an older child and can be under the misapprehension that this is pandering to a child's every whim. Let me say this. This is not mollycoddling. This is providing the foundation for a happy, regulated childhood. This is providing the missing link between trust and mistrust. The difference between secure attachment and poor attachment.

The answer is not to carry on regardless when children have significant gaps in their ability to regulate themselves. The answer is to go back to the beginning and do all the delightful, playful, soothing things you would do with a baby to bring out their trust, their social skills and their joyful emotions. Otherwise, we run the risk of children growing, without fully developing their capacity to regulate their own emotions or empathise with others. This is not something you will need to do with *all* children, but it is essential for children who have missed out.

Children with significant social and emotional delay

Bearing in mind the setbacks of the past few years, there are a lot more children presenting with social and

Children have Changed

emotional delay. It's understandable considering the context of the pandemic. However, there have always been children who experience significant delay in their emotional and social development. Often these children will go on to be diagnosed with conditions like Autism or ADHD. They may have been born prematurely or have underlying medical reasons for their delay. These children also need our support to help to regulate their emotions. For them, it's essential.

They probably won't be able to tell us how they are feeling and, in all honesty, we may never know how they are feeling, because some children may experience the physical world in a very different way to the way we experience it. When these children become dysregulated, it can be very difficult to find the cause. They can sometimes have long meltdowns that go on with no obvious cause and no apparent trigger. If you have a child who seems unable to regulate themself, all of the strategies in this chapter can still be used to support them, but I would also advise you to seek further health advice from the child's health visitor or GP.

Children have Changed

Chapter 3

Resolving Sleep Disturbance

I've Got One That Won't Even Come Out of
Their Pushchair!

Children have Changed

Children have Changed

A True Story.

*O*n a visit to a reception class in a busy, city centre school, I sat cross legged on the floor with the children as the teacher counted how many heads were in the circle today.

"Nineteen," she said brightly to the children. "For the moment," she whispered as an aside to me.

"For the moment?"

"They arrive in dribs and drabs all through the morning," she said rolling her eyes. "It's got worse over the past few years."

Sure enough, as the children went off to various activities, one child was hurriedly led in by a parent wearing a onesie, another parent in pyjamas and dressing gown dropped their dishevelled child off a bit later. A third child arrived mid-morning, looking like he'd just woken, hair on end and sleep in his eyes. He was ushered away, discreetly given a bowl of cereal and a school jumper was kindly pulled over his pyjama top.

I watched these children carefully as the day progressed. Despite there being lots of interesting areas to play in and activities on offer, they took longer to engage and they hung back. They'd missed the introduction to the day and looked completely lost

Children have Changed

at times. They played less and chatted less with other children. The most noticeable thing about all three of them was the number of times they yawned throughout the morning. Huge, wide gaping yawns.

"How often are they late?" I asked.

"Most days," shrugged their teacher. "We've tried incentives. Certificates for full attendance, that kind of thing, but they're only four. It's the parents that need to wake up and get them here. They're missing out."

She was genuinely angry on her children's behalf. She had a good point.

Sleep Disruption.

Many of the children I work with have disrupted sleep patterns. They can't seem to crack the code of understanding the rhythm of day and night, light and dark. They arrive looking washed out, listless, clinging onto comfort blankets or dummies for dear life. They're easily distressed, touchy and ill tempered. Their parents often have accompanying dark hollows under their eyes, sometimes struggling to string a sentence together.

There are many reasons for sleep disruption. Genuine medical conditions prevent some children finding a regular sleep pattern (more information on that later in this chapter). At the other end of the disrupted sleep

Children have Changed

spectrum are children with chaotic home lives where a bedtime routine just isn't a priority. Schools are trying to manage an increasing number of these children who are allowed to stay up late watching screens or gaming.

Add in to the mix some stark societal changes. I've recently met children with parents and grandparents who all share the same bed because they work shift patterns and "hot-bed" in between, meaning the whole extended family share one bedroom. I've chatted to parents who have to work long hours and so keep their child up later than they know is ideal, so they can at least have some quality time together before bedtime. I've also worked with a family who can't afford a bed for their child and so lay him to sleep on the sofa while family life has to carry on around him.

Social factors definitely play a detrimental part in disruptive sleep pattens. It's always worth getting to know your families and sensitively enquiring about living conditions, so we at least understand the reasons for some of our children's lack of zest in the morning.

Considerations for pandemic babies.

Although the sleep patterns of young children were studied during lockdown periods, a significant amount of change wasn't actually recorded. However, the ensuing Cost of living crisis and the Climate emergency have both infiltrated our children's lives since 2020.

Children have Changed

Teachers and headteachers often tell me there has been a shift in parent's perception of the importance sleep, of routine and of education in general. None of us ever expected to live through a pandemic, but since it occurred and we made it out alive, our collective psyche has shifted somewhat. What is the point in being punctual, hard-working, gaining an education and achieving qualifications if the world can be thrown into chaos at any future moment? If the icebergs are going to melt and we're all going to be washed out to sea, why not relax, enjoy life, take it easy while we can? This may seem facetious, but it does seem to be a pervading theme with some parents. Being late for school is no longer seen as such a big deal, in the same way that some parents don't worry about taking holidays in term time. Attitudes have slackened. If children stay up late, where's the harm?

Most Early years teachers would be able to tell you the harm …no holds barred.

How much sleep should we be getting?

Most of us don't get enough sleep in this twenty-four-hour world. There is too much temptation around us. Our culture is now firmly open around the clock. Long gone are Sunday rest days or city centre shops that shut at 5pm. TV used to end at midnight when I was a teenager. Now you can watch anything you want at any time of the day or night, be it gaming, internet shopping, gambling or streaming. Box-sets that

Children have Changed

display a countdown, suck us in to just one more episode before bed and tempt us up past bedtime. Shopping centres open later and later to cater to people who work longer hours, enticing us in, reminiscence of an ultra-fast paced Tokyo lifestyle. FOMO (Fear of missing out) happens even in young children.

The recommended hours of sleep for a pre-schooler (3 - 6 years) is 11-13 hours, according to NHS guidelines. This amount of sleep not only allows a child's body to regulate and recharge, it allows parents a well-earned wind down for the day. As Matthew Walker says in his book *Why We Sleep*,

"There does not seem to be one major organ within the body or process within the brain, that isn't optimally enhanced by sleep."

As adults we should be aiming for between seven to nine hours, but studies have proven most adults fall short too. (I know I regularly do). The importance and benefit of a good night's sleep are becoming more underrated than ever before.

How do children benefit from a good night sleep?

Sleep is a precious commodity for children. It helps to regulate all kinds of essential things including their mood, focus and appetite. Tired children are grumpy children. Common sense tells us that a tired brain can't concentrate. Attention span becomes reduced and our memory depleted. Tired children also lose their ability

Children have Changed

to empathise. As adults, we at least have the emotional regulation to slow down when we're tired, but children can fight against their own sleep impulse and paradoxically seem to speed up the more tired they become, with their behaviour becoming more and more erratic.

I used to fight sleep as a child and remember the feeling of being carried back to bed for the umpteenth time, growing more and more desperate to know what I was missing out on downstairs as my parents became more and more fed up with me. If only I'd known what I was doing to my concentration levels and capacity to learn.

Good quality sleep is key to:

- a healthy, regulated appetite.
- good concentration and memory, actually making us cleverer.
- a replenished immune system.
- regulated blood sugar as quality sleep fine tunes our insulin levels.
- prevention against depression and anxiety.
- improving our mood and making us feel happier for longer.
- improving our waistlines, leading to optimal weight.
- warding off disease.
- helping to maintain a healthy biome in our gut.

Children have Changed

○ providing a longer life span.

Just like adults, children need their full quota of quality sleep if they are to function properly, remain in good humour, and have zest, energy and creativity. To be able to work with early years children we also need to be lively, creative and passionate in our profession. You can't do that on poor quality sleep. You just can't. You may get away with it for an odd night, but poor-quality sleep steals our joy and passion for life.

Sleep disrupters.

There have always been children who reach the utopia of a good night sleep quicker than others. Some children, (of somewhat smug parents), go to bed on time, settle easily and wake up refreshed and energised in the morning. For other children a successful sleep pattern can take a lot longer to achieve and for a few parents, it must seem as though it will never happen as they drag themselves through another bleary-eyed day. Often there is no obvious cause for this. My three children all had different sleep patterns ranging from the sublime to the ridiculous, but were all brought up in a very similar way.

Once children find their feet and start toddling, they often settle better at night because of the energy they are expending in the day, but children who still experience severely disrupted sleep patterns when they have passed the toddling stage are usually

Children have Changed

referred to a pre-school specialist. Depending where you are located, this could be a paediatrician, an infant neurodevelopment team or a specialist nurse, all of whom will most likely offer a supported sleep programme.

Health considerations.

Over the pandemic, hospitals and health centres were unable to work with families face to face. For many parents, this meant that rather than visiting a clinic as an outpatient, they were offered support via a telephone or zoom call. It goes without saying, all health professionals did their best to continue to support families in a very difficult situation, they were following government guidance after all, but lockdown restrictions meant many children weren't seen in person. Unfortunately, this meant some children with significant delay, weren't picked up as early as they may have been because parents had to explain over the phone the difficulties they were experiencing.

Step into the shoes of a first-time parent in a lockdown situation for a moment. They had very limited contact with the outside world, zero parenting groups were operating, there was less contact with extended family and friends, face to face appointments were delayed or cancelled altogether and waiting lists grew longer and longer so they may not have actually had any face- to-face advice or support.

Children have Changed

New parents had limited, if any, first-hand comparisons with children the same age as their child. If their child was not reaching their expected milestones, parents quite legitimately, may not have realised and so not reported it to their health visitor. Issues like severe sleep disruption may not have been picked up until much later when waiting lists eventually started to reduce and children were once again assessed in person. On the other hand, parents who were understandably anxious about their child (and let's face it, who wouldn't be – we were in a goddam pandemic!) may have over-emphasised their concerns to health professionals over the phone.

There is no one to blame in this situation. Both anxious parents and blissfully unaware parents were all trying to do their best under a set of circumstances out of our control. We can only move forwards, taking into account the legacy of the pandemic. We need to keep talking about this because when we are planning for these children, we should consider that quite a number of children did not receive enough support to enable them to achieve a good sleep routine. The effect on these children's learning and mood is considerable and negative. It is also impacting on other children in our classrooms.

In the early years, children have busier brains that at any other time and they are making more neural pathways during these years than they will at any other point in their lives. Sleep is essential for the brain to be able to cope effectively with the amount of

Children have Changed

information that needs processing. Without good quality sleep, we can expect tantrums, bad moods and unwanted behaviours. Teachers know this only too well.

Case study: Molly's story.

Molly is a beautifully dressed, three-year-old little girl with an infectious smile and gorgeous bouncing curls that spring from her head. She has a significant delay in her speech, language and communication. Molly's parent Sara, is on the verge of exhaustion as she can't remember the last time Molly slept through the night.

During the pandemic, Molly and Sara were very isolated and Sara developed social anxiety. Consequently, they rarely visited the park or shops and barely left their flat. Sara did speak to several health professionals over the phone about Molly's disrupted sleep patterns, but she didn't see anyone face to face. When health and education services started to open up again, Sara felt too anxious to attend a face-to-face appointment for Molly and so they didn't attend the hospital appointment, meaning Molly was discharged.

Sara's health visitor recognised that the family needed support and managed to persuade Sara that a re-referral for Molly was needed, but Molly is now at the back of a very long waiting list. The health visitor also encouraged Sara to take Molly to a local nursery

Children have Changed

so she can start to develop interactions with other children. When Sara finally plucked up the courage to take her, Molly refused to get out of her pushchair. She wrapped herself in a blanket and curled into a ball, refusing to look at anyone. Sara left feeling more distressed than ever and was reluctant to return the next day.

Molly's attendance is still poor, but a very patient key worker has had some success at encouraging Sara to bring Molly in. When they arrive, she encourages Molly out of her pushchair, by using a familiar toy, and she sends Sara photographs to reassures her that Molly has stopped crying, but by mid- morning, Molly is usually either inconsolable again or fast asleep, neither of which are conducive states to learn in.

Molly is only too typical of children who have missed out on early face to face health interventions to help resolve sleep issues that have since grown into seemingly insurmountable problems, affecting children's education, relationships, interactions and all-round development.

Molly was lucky. She had an excellent health visitor who persisted in referring to children's services and she also provided emotional support in the form of a listening ear for Sara when she was feeling like she would never sleep through the night again. The referrals eventually resulted in Molly attending a specialist nursery placement where Molly started to gain some momentum and she is now managing to stay

Children have Changed

awake throughout the session. She is also beginning to allow familiar adults in to her space and she can communicate with single words. The power of kind and understanding practitioners never fails to amaze me.

(Molly is still waiting for a health appointment about her disrupted sleep).

Recipe for a good night sleep:

- o   It sounds obvious but rule out any discomfort. Could your child be hungry or thirsty? Is the temperature of the room too hot or too cold? Are they wet? Are their nightclothes scratchy?
- o   Avoid screens for at least 60 minutes before sleep as it is proven that they disrupt sleep patterns.
- o   Keep bedtime a consistent time every night.
- o   Have a bath with a few drops of lavender oil or a shower with lavender oil on a flannel.
- o   Warm a fluffy towel and warm your child's pyjamas.
- o   Give your child a warm drink of milk.
- o   Keep to a routine where teeth are cleaned for two minutes and your child goes to the toilet before bed.
- o   Share a story. This must be a real book, not a screen.

Children have Changed

- o Have a relaxed chat to recap the day's events and say what you are looking forward to tomorrow.
- o Give your child a good night kiss and hug.
- o Make sure their room is calm, quiet, cool and dark.
- o Have a clear expectation they will stay in bed and you'll see them in the morning.
- o Adopt a caring consistent, but firm approach. You expect your child to stay in bed because it's good for them to have a good night sleep. Be confident and expect them to settle. Your child will pick up their cues from you so be firm and authoritative (not authoritarian).
- o If they wake in the night, calmly put them back to bed with as little fuss as possible to avoid exciting them.

Medical reasons for Sleep disruption:

Apart from the usual common cold and childhood illnesses which may cause your child to wake in discomfort, if you have consistently used a bedtime routine similar to the one above and you are still experiencing sleepless nights with your child, there are certain medical conditions that can disrupt sleep:

Sleep Apnoea

Sleep apnoea can be caused by enlarged adenoids (nodules located at the back of the throat, behind the

Children have Changed

nose). One of my own daughters had very enlarged tonsils and adenoids and would snore unbelievably loudly for a four-year-old, followed by her seeming to hold her breath for an eternity before the snoring kicked in again.

This meant that for a long time, I didn't sleep properly either. I would lie awake anxiously waiting for her breathing to kick back in. When she had her tonsils and adenoids removed, she started sleeping like a log (as did I) and her concentration, memory and mood all improved. Children prone to runny noses and allergies can also have problems sleeping. It's less common for medical practitioners to remove adenoids and tonsils today, but if you are concerned your child may have sleep apnoea, visit your GP and get help.

Nightmares

Nightmares (sometimes called night terrors) happen during the stage of sleep when your child's brain is very active, known as the REM stage. You may notice your child's eyes moving rapidly behind their closed eyes. No-one knows for sure why nightmares occur, but common triggers can include a new baby in the family, moving house, starting a new school or a trauma such as a family breakup. Children can also be very vulnerable to watching something on screen that they find upsetting, remembering that they haven't yet developed the same coping strategies that we have to deal with frightening scenes and their dreams can be

Children have Changed

very vivid. This happened when one of my own children were young and they watched the movie Jurassic Park!

If your child has a nightmare, reassure them that you are there and nothing bad is going to happen. Explain it was a bad dream but it can't hurt you and once you have woken up, it goes away. Comfort your child with a cuddle and let them know everyone has bad dreams from time to time. For young children, you might want to use a "night spray." (An atomizer bottle of water) to spray their room against bad things like witches or whatever it is they have had a bad dream about. A night light can also provide reassurance if they wake in the night.

Sleep walking

Sleep walking is less common but can occur for many of the same reasons nightmares occur. There is no specific treatment for sleepwalking, but it is helpful to follow the above recipe for a good night's sleep and make sure your child's routine is consistent and relaxed. If a child is waking at the same time every night to sleepwalk, you could try gently waking them 15 to 20 minutes before they would normally sleepwalk to try and alter their sleep pattern.

Bed wetting

If you are going through the process of toileting your child, a few accidents are perfectly normal. To avoid accidents at night, don't give your child drinks containing caffeine (Cola, tea or coffee) before bed as

Children have Changed

this can make accidents more likely to happen. Opt instead for a warm milk drink and make sure they have used the toilet or potty just before bed. Most children will wet the bed at some stage, so if this does happen, reassure your child calmly that it's just an accident and accidents happen to everyone.

Don't try to prevent accidents by waking your child or carrying them to the toilet in the night as this can make the problem worse in the long term. If bedwetting becomes a regular occurrence, speak to your health visitor or GP. Waterproof covers are a godsend if your child has frequent accidents. Keep a potty next to their bed or make sure they can easily get to the toilet and give plenty of praise when they do have a dry night.

Bruxism
Bruxism, or grinding teeth in your sleep, is reported in about twenty per cent of children up to the age of eleven years but can often be over-looked or misdiagnosed. Bruxism is a sleep disorder but it can also occur as a response to other sleep disorders, for example, it's more common in children who already have sleep apnoea and tend to mouth breathe. It's also more common in children with dental problems, children who suffer with headaches or joint pain and can also be related to stress, anxiety disorders and hyperactivity.

Snoring and mouth breathing are not always considered significant by parents, so bruxism can be missed and not be reported early. If you think your

Children have Changed

child may be grinding their teeth to the point it is disrupting their sleep pattern, visit your GP.

Bruxism.org.uk has plenty more information.

Restless Legs Syndrome

Restless legs syndrome, also known as Willis-Ekbom disease, is a movement disorder that can significantly disturb a child's sleep. The main symptom is a painless but overwhelming urge to move your legs which often increases at night. Restless legs syndrome may be caused by an underlying issue such as iron deficiency. (Iron deficiency is common in UK children and is associated with several negative outcomes, including adverse effects on cognitive and behavioural development). In certain cases, the cause of restless legs may be genetic. This disorder is largely under-diagnosed in children.

If your child is experiencing an uncontrollable urge to move their legs that gets worse at night and disrupts their sleep, consult your GP as if properly diagnosed, symptoms can be treated.

Medical conditions

Children with long-term illnesses or additional needs can often find it more difficult to sleep through the night which can be challenging both for parent and child. Always talk to your health visitor or GP if you need further advice, or make an appointment at a sleep clinic if you are lucky enough to have one in your area.

Children have Changed

Sleep Medication

Giving a child medication to sleep is a big decision and should be carefully considered. Melatonin is sometimes prescribed to children who can't seem to settle and don't give their parents any respite. It can often support a child to get to sleep, but in my experience, won't necessarily keep them asleep all night. Many parents tell me they wouldn't cope without it.

But before we consider medication, there are known sleep disrupters that we can rule out:

- o Caffeine is present in tea, coffee (including de-caffeinated versions) hot chocolate, energy drinks and chocolate so always try to eliminate these from a child's diet as far as possible. Caffeine stays in an adult's system for up to eight hours; longer for children. It can interfere significantly with sleep patterns.

- o Poor diet can be another factor in sleep disruption and is often a vicious circle with one impacting the other, as tired children can either lose their appetite or overeat to compensate for the hormones that kick in when we become tired.

Children have Changed

- o Stress and anxiety often play a large part in keeping children awake, even in very young children so try to talk through any anxieties your child may have.

- o Screen time or the blue light effect can significantly and negatively impact a child's sleep patterns.

Further support and resources:

- o The charity Contact has more information about helping you and your child sleep.

- o Scope also has sleep advice for parents of disabled children.

- o Sleepcharity.org.uk has lots of useful information

- o Infant Sleep Information Service (ISIS)

- o Millpond sleep programme offers online training courses for parents and practitioners.

Children have Changed

Chapter 4

The Effect of Diet on Learning.

His Mum Says He'll Only Eat Wotsits!

Children have Changed

Children have Changed

Case study: Jack's story.

*J*ack is four years old. He lives with his Mum, Dana in a small apartment. Dana is unemployed at the moment and the budget in their household is extremely limited. Jack often arrives in school having had no breakfast, but because his mum doesn't work, he isn't entitled to attend the free breakfast club. When he arrives, the teacher often takes him aside and gives him a bowl of cereal, regardless of meal times, as she knows how hard he finds it to concentrate on an empty tummy.

Jack enjoys his free school meal at lunchtime (an entitlement for all children in Wales). He often has second helpings. The lunchtime supervisors all appreciate his healthy appetite. In the evening, Jack usually has either a paste sandwich or bag of crisps until the next day. Dana has sometimes resorted to food banks, but she hates the stigma attached and would rather not use them if she can help it.

Jack is often fidgety, unfocussed and tired in school. His learning outcomes are low for his age. Dana carries a huge amount of guilt about Jack as she doesn't think he is getting the right vitamin balance for a growing boy, but feels powerless to do anything about it.

Children have Changed

Pandemic diets

If you ask most people if their diet changed during the pandemic, the likelihood is they will say no, or if it did change, it was in a positive way. For more affluent families, there was more time to sit together as a family, more time to prepare meals from scratch. A national epidemic of traditional soda bread and banana bread baking was going on and there was a surge in the sales of baking ingredients. It felt like a return to the good old days for some of us. There was an anxious couple of weeks when food and toilet roll shortages threatened to impact us, but thankfully it didn't last and supermarket shelves were soon stocked again. But during those anxious days of social distancing, it was the role of the delivery van that gained speed and momentum like nothing else.

The rise of takeaway deliveries

Anyone who needed to self-isolate was much more likely to use supermarket home delivery services and it was during the pandemic that this relatively new phenomenon really gained momentum. Restaurant and fast-food franchises started to increase their deliveries, in a bid to remain sustainable in the days where customers were scarce at best, non-existent at worst. Meals on wheels stepped up a gear to support the old and immobile. The UK delivery culture changed.

Children have Changed

Since society opened back up, this lessened a little, but one of the unexpected legacies of the pandemic was an explosion in takeaway delivery. Since 2022 Deliveroo, Uber-Eats and Just Eat are the front runners.

Just Eat was originally launched in Denmark in 2001, but the Danes have far less inclination for take-away food than the British, so they made their fortune over here. Incidentally, the UK is responsible for a massive 50% of the European food market. You only have to walk along your local high street to see a huge increase in delivery bikes collecting McDonalds, Dominoes, Pizza Hut. Even Greggs, the largely pastry based high street bakery, now has a market net worth of 2.82 billion as of February 2024.

We are becoming increasingly reliant on ready prepared and delivered meals. Teachers have even noticed a rise in some children having their breakfast delivered from McDonalds before they get to school. Children's diets are often perceived to be better quality than in the past. After the second world war, for example, rationing was still in place for much of the 1950's and children's diets were meagre and limited, but were they really less healthy than today's sugar and salt laden takeaways?

Healthy role models

Sometimes, we have to take a long hard look at ourselves and own up to our own unhealthy dietary

Children have Changed

habits. Attitudes to food can be emotive in different ways for all of us. We eat for comfort, when we are feeling tired, emotional, a bit down or if we are feeling anxious about something. We use sugar because it gives us a buzz, a hit of adrenaline or because we're addicted to it. Chocolate also contains hidden caffeine and is addictive.

We use food to celebrate: birthdays, anniversaries, festivals, Valentine's Day, Fridays, Saturdays and Sundays. (I certainly fall into this category). We are a nation of overeaters. Fast food loaded with salt, fat and sugar is more popular than ever, even though there is more guidance available about the importance of healthy eating than ever.

The Health Survey for England 2021 estimates that over a quarter (25.9%) of adults in England are obese and a further 37.9% are overweight but not obese. Obesity being defined as having a body mass index (BMI) of 30 or above. Recently, there are calls in the scientific community to get rid of BMI as it can be inaccurate so we need to bear in mind that your BMI is only one measure and genetics and environmental factors can also come into play.

However, we need to stop and look around. We are children's greatest role models and many of us are, if not obese, overweight. There's no getting away from it - children copy what adults do. It's no use saying do as I say. Children are more perceptive than that. For young children, adults are heroes. They want to be just

Children have Changed

like their parents and teachers. If they watch us taking pleasure in the wrong foods too often, they will want the wrong foods themselves.

I'm pretty sure you already know the components of a healthy diet, and even if you're not sure, you have only to type it into google to find great advice and graphics such as MyPlate showing the array of rainbow of foods we are all supposed to be eating, but are we really role modelling this?

Diet and brain development.

Jamie Oliver raised our collective awareness of a link between poor nutrition and academic attainment, all the way back in 2005 when he filmed his upgrading of the shocking school meals in a secondary school, later rolling out his successful healthy school meals more widely. Since then, we have government funded Healthy school programmes to continue the fight, but it's an ongoing battle.

Positive measures include Scotland's government now offering free meals to all primary 1-5 classes. In Wales, all primary school children now get free school meals. England is committed, at least until 2025, to providing free school meals to its most disadvantaged pupils. Yet plenty of young children still aren't getting the nutrition they need to be able to focus properly. Interestingly, Finland, the country that is a regular front runner in the PISA attainment charts, offers all children a free healthy school meal and makes no

Children have Changed

distinction between disadvantaged and advantaged children.

Most fast food obviously contains lots more empty calories than basic home cooked food. Those high levels of salt, fat and sugar are directly linked to poor attention. They change the chemicals and neurotransmitters in our children's brains.

Children are doing their best, but they are sometimes running on empty, even if they have eaten. Fast food of the fried variety doesn't provide the nutrition children deserve to be able to function properly. No wonder they get fidgety, overtired, easily distracted, bad tempered. No wonder there is an increase in laxatives prescribed to the under-fives and toilet training is more challenging than ever. (more on this later).

We've all either heard of, or experienced for ourselves the cost-of-living crisis and can see the rising pressures on families. Breakfast clubs are doing wonders to give children a fighting chance of being able to focus once their tummies are full, especially those that offer protein rich breakfasts. Children need good nutrition for physical growth, energy, brain development and to achieve quality sleep. It's essential. We all know how we should avoid giving children cakes, biscuits, chips, sweets, processed meat and takeaway foods high in saturated fat, sugar and salt.

Children have Changed

Insidious advertising

…And yet it's still happening. The pandemic is over. We no longer need to rely on take-away deliveries as we might if we were self-isolating or categorised as being vulnerable, yet those take-away franchises have gone on to become some of the UK's more profitable businesses. They run highly successful advertising campaigns, constantly reminding and luring our tired selves towards full fat, fully salted nirvana.

Advertisements on billboards, buses, bus shelters and TV campaigns tempt us into the must have, next level of burger or twist on fried chicken at the click of an app. It could be argued that fast food is not aimed at a children's market, but it is in full view of our young children and they have eyes. It's definitely not easy to stay strong and resist this tempting level of assault, however well informed we are, especially when you add a child's pester power on top.

Case study: Shiv's story

Shiv is five years old. Her parents both work for long hours. Shiv's Mum Fiona is a teacher and Shiv's Dad, Rob is a train driver. They tend to shop online, a habit they developed in lockdown as Fiona has Type 2 diabetes and was self-isolating.

Fiona and Rob try to make sure Shiv has a good breakfast before she leaves the house in the morning, but they often leave so early that Shiv doesn't want to eat yet, so they rely on breakfast club where Shiv

Children have Changed

usually gets cereal and toast. In the evening, they try to cook something healthy, but if Fiona has work commitments like parent evenings or reports to write, they often resort to takeaways or ready meals. The family almost always have a take-away on Friday and Saturday. They try to counteract this by driving Shiv to a dance class on Saturday afternoon so she can burn off some energy.

Although Shiv looks an average weight for her five years, and seemingly has lots of energy her parents were shocked recently when she was assessed as being in the obese category at her five-year health assessment.

Childhood obesity

Obesity rates in children are shockingly high in the UK. Childhood obesity data is gathered as part of the National Child Measurement Programme which is usually carried out in schools when children are in their reception year. According to the House of Commons report, the obesity rate in reception children decreased from 10.1% in 2021/22 to 9.2% compared with the highest ever recorded figure in 2020/21 of 14.4%.

This does still mean the majority of reception pupils are a healthy weight, but for those children already recorded as obese, there is more bad news, because the prevalence of severe obesity is more than three times higher in the most deprived areas (3.8%) compared

Children have Changed

with those living in the least deprived areas. Children living in areas of deprivation are twice as likely to be obese as their more affluent peers.

There is a clear link between childhood obesity and disrupted sleep. It's a bit of a chicken and egg situation because a lack of sleep can lead to childhood obesity and those children who get less than their recommended hours of sleep are more at risk of developing obesity according to a study by the University of Warwick. One of the co-authors, Dr Michelle Miller, Reader of Biochemical Medicine, Health Sciences, Warwick Medical School said:

"Being overweight can lead to cardiovascular disease and type-2-diabetes which is also on the increase in children. The findings of the study indicate that sleep may be an important potentially modifiable risk factor (or marker) of future obesity."

The National Child Measurement Programme is the UK tool used to identify childhood obesity but some children are given a diagnosis of obese without actually appearing to look like our typical image of an overweight child. Furthermore, parents don't often receive any explanation with this diagnosis when it is presented to them and can often be dismissive of it. They can't understand how their child can be obese if they fit into average size clothes for their age and look a typical weight.

117

Children have Changed

Education and context are both key here. Parents need more information so their awareness of their child's body mass index (BMI) is understood. They need to know the future consequences of not adapting their child's diet so they are not oblivious to avoiding the nasties potentially lurking in their infant's body. However, we need to stay aware of the fact that these tests are carried out on growing children. The NHS website agrees that it can be difficult to tell if your child is overweight when they are still growing, but they do have a handy online calculator to check body mass index (BMI) on a regular basis. You just need to enter your child's date of birth, height and weight.

https://www.nhs.uk/health-assessment-tools/calculate-your-body-mass-index/calculate-bmi-for-children-teenagers/

The importance of hydration.

Hydration is easy to overlook, but can make a huge difference to children's wellbeing. Most health visitors and Healthy School Programmes advise that children should only be given water or milk and until they are at least two years old, and children should drink whole milk, not the semi skimmed or skimmed variety. Fizzy drinks, squash and fruit juice should be completely avoided, according to the NHS, as children who drink a lot of sugary drinks are more likely to be overweight or obese. The sugars contained in fizzy drinks also

Children have Changed

interact with bacteria in a child's mouth to form acid, which is responsible for tooth decay, and that goes for the sugar free versions too.

There has been an increase in children entering schools recently with delayed self-help skills, such as drinking out of a bottle or sippy cup. The longer we leave weaning a child from a bottle, the more comfort they can attach to it, so soon after their first birthday is a good time to start introducing an open cup. It may be a bit hap hazard at first, but an open cup is better for teeth development and ultimately, for independence.

The importance of protein.

If you have a child struggling with their concentration and attention, it's worth thinking about the importance protein can play, especially if it's eaten earlier in the day. Children who have hyperactive tendencies can particularly benefit here, as eating good quality sources of protein can help to raise levels of an amino acid called tyrosine, which in turn can boost a child's serotonin and dopamine (lovely, feel-good hormones). This helps to regulate energy, mental focus, emotions and even reduce anxiety.

A protein snack or breakfast could include:

- o good quality sausages,
- o humous and vegetable dips,
- o peanut butter on crackers or toast,

Children have Changed

- o turkey and cucumber rolls,
- o ham and cheese cubes.

There are many breakfast clubs doing great work and choosing to provide protein over the traditional carbohydrate-heavy cereal and toast. Protein actually prevents surges in blood sugar which are known to heighten hyperactivity and impulsivity, something teachers are reporting as on the increase. In making this small change, teachers are noticing a marked change in some children's behaviour.

Is a vegan diet suitable for young children?

In 2021, while we were still getting used to the new normal, the Climate Change Committee advised that people should reduce meat eating, not only for their health, but also for the planet. Production of meat worldwide is responsible for a third of all greenhouse gas emissions. This information has gained momentum with several high-profile Netflix documentaries recently promoting a vegan lifestyle and there has been a significant increase in vegetarianism and veganism in the UK.

According to the Independent, when surveyed, more than twenty per cent of children are either already vegan or would like to become vegan. BBC Good Food found that eight per cent of children aged between five and sixteen are already following a vegan diet and thirteen per cent were vegetarian in 2021. It's

Children have Changed

a question I'm sometimes asked by parents' keen to do the right thing for their young child, both morally and nutritionally. The key is, whichever lifestyle you choose, meals need to be properly planned if you are going to achieve the best nutrition.

The British Medical Journal states that studies have shown when children follow a healthy vegan diet, they have normal growth rates, lower fat mass, lower blood cholesterol and lower fasting glucose levels. They also have higher intakes of fibre, vitamin C and many other beneficial nutrients, compared to their counterparts following a meat-eating diet who can consume higher than recommended amounts of saturated fat, sugar and insufficient fibre.

It's well documented that a vegan adult diet significantly reduces the risk of some types of cancer as well as type 2 diabetes (of which over ten per cent of our young children are already potential candidates for at their five-year health check). There is no definitive evidence that when started in the early years, a vegan diet guarantees lasting health benefits but if you are interested in more information on following a vegan diet with your child, this book is a good place to start:

Feeding Your Vegan Child written by NHS dietitian Sandra Hood, who herself has been vegan for over 30 years and raised a vegan family.

Children have Changed

Always consult your GP or health visitor if you are considering making significant changes to your child's diet.

Promoting health / subliminal messages

Role modelling a healthy and active lifestyle, in my opinion, is the most positive thing we can do as parents and teachers. Try not to pressure children into eating all the food on their plate if they don't want to. Being too controlling around food can unintentionally lead to children using unhealthy foods, later on in life, to manage negative emotions.

Instead, try to consider factors that influence our attitudes to food and the messages we are passing on to our children. Do you promise sweets as a reward for good behaviour? Could you promise a play on the local park instead? Do your children hear you commenting on the weight increase of celebrities or do you consciously give body positive messages? We have all received subliminal messages about food and weight ourselves. It's only by recognising and being aware that we can break unhealthy cycles.

How long should parents breastfeed?

I'm not a health practitioner, and you should always ask your own GP, health visitor or paediatrician for advice but in my own recent experience of working with young families and children, I've noticed many mothers are breast feeding their child to a later age and

Children have Changed

it's becoming more common for three and even four-year-old's to still be breast fed. Sometimes, mums are anxious and unsure when to stop but there is little research evidence around this topic. NHS guidance states:

There's no reason why you should not continue breastfeeding your child into their 2nd year and beyond. You and your toddler can continue to enjoy the benefits of breastfeeding for as long as you want to and your toddlers may also find breastfeeding comforting when they're ill or upset. - NHS website.

Are there any enhanced benefits for a child to continue to breastfeed past 12 months? According to breastfeeding expert Amy Spangler in *Breastfeeding: A Parent's Guide*, breast milk can provide up to one-third of the calorie, protein, and calcium needs of a toddler. This can be especially beneficial if the child is refusing to eat other foods due to illness. Spangler also found that toddler illnesses are shorter in duration due to breast milk continuing to create illness-specific antibodies. Extended nursing can also provide comfort to the child and help with bonding.

However, breastfeeding over the age of one year has been linked to an increase in dental cavities, most likely due to inadequate oral hygiene and night-time feeds. (source: Michigan school of public health).

Children have Changed

Children with sensory issues around food.

Almost all children will go through a fussy phase at some point in their development. This can happen at any age and is best dealt with calmly and sensibly, by continuing to offer healthy choices, making sure they get plenty of fresh air and exercise so they have a healthy appetite and not giving in to demands for sweets or snacks in between regular meal times.

However, some children, particularly children with a sensory processing disorder or children who have been medically peg fed in the past, (fed through an intravenous feeding tube) may genuinely struggle to eat new foods. They may experience the different colours, smells, textures and tastes of certain foods in a different way to us and will need plenty of time and patience to build up their tolerance and trust. I have included some tips below that I've seen work really well, but always follow the advice of your dietician or health practitioner first, if your child has feeding issues.

Building up tolerance

If your child has a very limited or restricted diet, try offering a separate bowl next to their plate with a small amount of the food that you would like them to try. For example, if your child will only eat chips and fishfingers, place those on their plate, but put a small amount of peas in a separate bowl near their plate. Do this every mealtime without fail.

Children have Changed

Don't expect this to work immediately. It may take several weeks of seeing that same bowl at mealtimes, but gradually, you may notice your child touching the bowl, then they may touch the peas, they may bring a pea to their lips and hopefully, finally put it into their mouth. This is all about slowly building up their tolerance and trust.

If your child is reluctant to try different textures and has a limited diet, you can also try building up their sensory tolerance through messy play with food. Play with cooked spaghetti, rainbow rice or make some marks in a tray of yoghurt.

Tips on positive nutrition for young children:

I'm as guilty as anyone of consuming the wrong foods (and drinks) and would never claim that this is easy. There are pressures and temptations from society all around us but you don't have to change everything, all at once. Making one small change is better than no change at all and can often lead to another change.

- o Be aware of and get savvy about food advertising campaigns. Choose to watch channels without tempting food adverts or turn the TV off during the advert breaks.

- o Limit takeaways to special occasions and instead make healthier fake-a-way versions.

Children have Changed

o If you work in a school or childcare facility, make children's diet a priority. Have a clear policy and get your parents involved in its development.

o Consider giving your child a vitamin B12 supplement if their diet doesn't include red meat. (Holland and Barat and Amazon both sell child supplements of V B12).

o Consider giving your child a multi vitamin supplement, especially if they are a fussy eater. If they won't take tablets there are other versions such as gummy chews and drops. For families on low incomes, ask your health visitor about schemes to receive free child vitamins.

o At least once a day, try to have a family mealtime together, where everyone gets involved in preparing the food, with no screen distractions.

o Setting the table can develop counting out skills and sorting and matching skills. Cooking and baking together have the potential to develop all kinds of science concepts like understanding how foods can change, mathematical concepts like weighing and measuring and language skills, like talking together and following instructions.

Children have Changed

o Being outdoors cannot be overrated. Fresh air and exercise (even walking) builds a healthy appetite and promotes good sleep.

o Provide plenty of milk and water and don't offer alternatives.

o Wean your child from a bottle and sippy cup as soon as possible to avoid teeth disruption and tooth decay.

o For children over two, swap to semi-skimmed milk.

o Don't give your child adult sized portions. Use a smaller plate.

o Growing fruit and vegetables, even if it's only some pots on a windowsill, can help to encourage your child to try new foods as well as start to understand where their food comes from.

o Choosing a healthy lifestyle and being a role model yourself is the best way to encourage children to make healthy choices.

o If you have a fussy eater, don't stop offering healthy foods, just because they are refusing them at the moment. Continue to offer small amounts and don't make a big deal about it if

Children have Changed

they do refuse. If you can, role model how tasty you find the food.

o   Consider giving children who are constantly on the go and have limited attention a fish oil supplement. A human brain is nearly sixty per cent fat. Replenishing the supply of omega 3 through eating plenty of oily fish or by using a supplement can support the functions of brain neuro transmitters and support positive behaviour.

o   Please be aware if your child is already taking medication, you should consult your doctor before giving them supplements (you can continue to eat oily fish regardless).

o   Turn off your smartphone. Recent research highlights the use of smartphones during meal times increases the number of calories eaten by both children and adults. The distraction of the screen can interfere with our physiological signals of hunger and cause us to overeat. (source - NIH National library of medicine).

Children like Jack (in the case study at the beginning of this chapter) are powerless over their situation. If they don't get the right nutrition their behaviour and consequently their learning will suffer. They need

Children have Changed

sustenance or their brains quite literally can't function properly.

Children have Changed

Chapter 5

Advice on Self-Help Skills (Including Toileting).

I Should be Teaching, Not Changing Nappies!

Children have Changed

Children have Changed

The issue that seems to cause the most consternation, following the pandemic, is the rise in children starting school without being toilet trained. What *is* going on out there?

A rise in children who are delayed in toileting.

Headteachers and teachers are angry and vocal about this, caught between the duties of the 2010 equality act and the rising tide of parents who have not managed to toilet train their child before they start school. Schools and settings need to balance the child's right to dignity, the parent's right to go to work without being called back to change their child, and the teachers' right to be able to teach as they've done in the past without changing a constant line of nappies. It's the area of delay I most get asked for help with and the reason I unwittingly gained the flattering title *Toilet Lady!*

'*I didn't become a teacher to change nappies,*" is a phrase only too familiar to me.

Twenty years ago, it was the norm for the majority of children to be toileted by three years old. It was expected that parents would get their child out of nappies and into *big girl or boy pants* before their first term in school. Schools insisted on it.

Of course, there would be some accidents. We have to expect three-year-olds to have days where they're too tired, too poorly, or simply too busy and forget

Children have Changed

themselves for a moment to remember about the toilet. No self-respecting Nursery teacher would expect anything else of their children. Children with medical conditions would of course be exempt from this expectation. But recently, something has shifted. Something fundamental, across society.

Increasing numbers of children are starting school in pull-ups or nappies and teachers are angry. They are passing that anger up and headteachers are also angry on their behalf. I don't believe for one minute that Nursery teachers are angry because they are too proud or feel above changing an occasional nappy.

They are angry because this is no longer occasional. It is having a detrimental effect on the learning opportunities of all children in the setting. Adult to child ratios change when children reach the age of three. Usually, at three, one adult is allocated to every eight children, compared to one adult to four children with two-year-olds. That ratio is in place because the expectation is children will be developing their self-help skills by the time they reach three, including being able to use the toilet independently.

Every time a nappy change happens, it pulls the adults away from the learning environment. It slows momentum in the classroom. There is less time to develop skills like following instructions, solving problems, learning about numeracy, reading books together and learning to share. Teachers are angry on behalf of their children because every nappy change put limits on other precious opportunities.

Children have Changed

Some of those children in nappies are more than capable of being independent. Teachers are angry because those children are not afforded the dignity they deserve. Classrooms are not set up for nappy changing and it can become very undignified in some circumstances with no specific changing area, little privacy, piles of dirty nappies to dispose of, not to mention the thinning patience of the teacher. I've come across several practitioners leaving the profession recently, due to the increase in changes they've had to do every session.

What are self-help skills?

It's not just toileting skills that are delayed. The full gamut of children's self-help skills lag behind where they used to be. Those skills we all need in life to be able to look after ourselves and keep ourselves healthy and safe. In the Early years, these include:
- Dressing and undressing
- Washing your hands and face
- Cleaning your teeth
- Brushing your hair
- Blowing your own nose and sneezing into your elbow
- Holding and manipulating a spoon and fork to feed yourself
- Drinking independently from an open cup
- Pouring your own drink
- Going to the toilet independently and washing your hands afterwards

Children have Changed

- o Carrying your own things and putting your toys away.
- o Putting your shoes on, tying laces, fastening buttons and zips.

That's not an exhaustive list, but you get the idea. We're trying to encourage children to be as independent as possible. Independence is the ultimate goal of early years practitioners and parents alike. When our children are eventually, truly independent and can stand on their own two feet, we have done our job. We've cracked it and should pop open the champagne to celebrate.

Independence is way more important than academic grades, because if anything happens to us, if our children have developed true independence they can look after themselves and keep themselves safe and healthy. It's how we ensure the survival of our human species. The more independence children develop, earlier in life, the less time we need to spend doing things for them, so leaving more time in the day to learn about other more exciting things.

Another true story: Physical Education with Nursery.

In the stone age, when I taught Nursery, we were lucky enough to have some allocated hall time to practice physical skills. As an overly keen, newly qualified teacher, I marched the children down to the

Children have Changed

school hall with their brand new, whiter than white first day of the year P.E. kits. Two adults to sixteen children. My patient Nursery Nurse trouped along at the end of the line, probably inwardly despairing at my optimism.

"Shoes, off," I said, at least sixteen times, frantically undoing buckles and triple knotted laces.

"Socks off", I said thirty-two times, encouraging little boys to tug at their toes. They looked back at me hopelessly, as if I'd lost the plot

"Jumpers off, over your head," I sounded like I had a stutter I said it that many times. Most children sat waiting with their arms in the air. A few got bored and zoomed in circuits around the hall. "Fold your clothes into a pile," I said with the false cheeriness of the doomed. God, it was stressful, but finally, finally, all sixteen of my little soldiers were in brilliant white T-shirts and shorts, ready to run and keep fit.

"Find a space," I said. My Nursery Nurse must have smirked at that one because everyone working in early years knows three year olds have no spacial awareness. But it didn't matter. There was no time to find a space. The whole hour had been taken up getting changed. As the bell went for home time, we went back to class, shivering in our PE kits.

The lesson here was for me of course, not the children. Young children need self-help tasks to be broken down into manageable chunks. This is sometimes referred to as back-chaining. After my first disastrous P.E. lesson, we worked on just taking off

Children have Changed

shoes and then moved onto socks and shoes for at least a term, slowly building up to full kits by the end of the year. The receiving Reception teacher could at least then manage to get some physical exercise in her P.E. lesson the following year.

Infant teachers have always focused on self-help skills. This is nothing new. Self-help skills take time to develop, but putting the time and effort in buys us more time later, and in education, time is a very precious commodity with all the demands of the curriculum. Self-help skills also buy children something much more important than time: their dignity, independence, confidence and self-esteem are all improved as they meet these important milestones.

Considerations for Pandemic babies

Being at home during lockdowns worked well for some families. It meant they had the luxury of additional time to play with and toilet train their child. For other families, they missed out on parenting groups, extended family visiting or informal conversations with other parents and didn't realise how or when they should start toileting. Children have clearly missed out on socialisation skills and as it's often claimed that children learn more from other children than they do from adults, in this light, self-help skills have been severely impacted.

Children have Changed

There are sometimes good reasons why a child isn't toiled trained by the time they start school. Where their birthday falls in the calendar is one. If a child is born in September, they will have almost a year more than a child with an August birthday to work on their toileting skills and are almost always more confident in going to the toilet independently.

When I taught Nursery, we used to display the children's birthdays, firstly so we could celebrate them, (You only get one chance in life to be four) but secondly, the adults in the room were reminded who was likely to need more time to develop skills. Younger children will undoubtedly have more accidents than their older peers and that's fine. It's all part of the learning process. In fact, almost all children have slip ups from time to time. Nursery teachers understand and accommodate for this brilliantly. However, the rising number of children who are still firmly in pull-ups is worrying.

For children with additional learning needs the speed they learn new skills can take a lot longer. A small percentage of children will also have valid medical reasons for toileting delay.

What is the cost of postponing toileting until a later age?

The last study that looked at the environmental impact of disposable nappies on our environment was in 2006, (eighteen years ago). The Environment

Children have Changed

Agency is the leading public body protecting and improving the environment in England and Wales has the job of ensuring our air, land and water are looked after by everyone in today's society, so that tomorrow's generations inherit a cleaner, healthier world.

In 2001, between two and three per cent of our household waste was estimated to be disposable nappies, approximately 400,000 tonnes of waste each year. That was based on the average age of a child being toilet trained at two and a half. But with more and more children entering our schools in nappies, aged three years plus, and the year-on-year rise in population in the UK, that figure will be much higher. A conservative estimate is 1.7 million children are in nappies at any one time in the UK.

There is an alternative to disposable nappies, which reduces demand on landfill but let's face it, reusable nappies are nowhere near as convenient for busy working parents and they also have an impact on the environment in other ways such as the water and energy used in washing and drying them. Unless you are washing them by hand (Urrgh!) or on a very low energy machine cycle, drying them outside and reusing them with a second child, they also add considerably to our carbon footprint.

There is no getting away from it, both types of nappies create environmental impact. Big steps forward have been made in the material disposable

Children have Changed

nappies are made from. They are lighter and more environmentally friendly than ever before and their impact on global warming has decreased slightly, but with children spending longer in them, the strides forward we've made in the materials they are made of are being undone by children wearing them for longer than they need to. All nappies damage our planet. The earlier we can get children out of them, the better.

Case study: Charlie's story.

Charlie is a little girl with heaps of energy, dimples, brown eyes and a beautiful wide smile. She has been in playgroup for almost six months and is going to start nursery school next term. She has recently turned three. Charlie is a quiet little girl but she likes to watch the other children and occasionally takes part in a little bit of pretend play with them. She loves rocking the dolls to sleep in the home corner and playing in the mud kitchen outside. She enjoys climbing on the climbing frame and peddling the bikes. Charlie still wears pull-ups.

In playgroup, the staff have noticed that before she soils herself, she finds a quiet place and hides herself away. When the other children go to the toilet, she has been spotted watching them. Sometimes, when she is uncomfortable, she will say "nappy wet," and last week she brought her own nappy bag to the changing mat. Despite these observations of Charlie's growing awareness, Charlie's mum says that Charlie is showing no signs of being ready at home.

Children have Changed

After playgroup, Charlie goes to another Nursery where she stays until 5.30pm when her mum picks her up. The staff at Charlie's afternoon childcare placement have also noticed signs that Charlie is ready.

Why are so many more children in nappies later?

Charlie has got all the signs of being ready to be toileted, but this is a classic example of modern life getting in the way. Potty training takes time, and time is often in very short supply for many young families. It also takes patience. The days when parents could stay at home to deal with accidents for a few weeks as you tried to catch your child with the potty have gone for many families. Working parents leave the house early and get home late. This is essential to pay the bills and keep a roof over their heads and good on them for doing it, but it means family routines are tighter and less flexible.

The thought of their child having accidents as they try to plough on in work can be overwhelming. Most families have two working parents these days and modern life can feel like a hamster wheel. There is less time to let children simply try being without a nappy and experience the feeling of air against skin. Coordinating potty training across a few different childcare settings is definitely not easy.

Another barrier to toilet training is the amazing advances in the quality of nappies and pull-ups. They

Children have Changed

are more discreet, absorbent, leak proof and comfortable than ever before. That all sounds great, except they are *so* comfortable, children forget that they are wearing them. The absorbency means they don't actually feel the sensation of wetness against their skin. That's great for skin, but no so great for learning about controlling your bladder and bowels. There's less reason to wake in the night if you don't feel wet and uncomfortable, but on the other hand, children are not learning the signals that tell their brain when they need to pee and what feeling wet feels like. A good tip is to put a pair of pants underneath the pull-ups and see if your child starts to notice.

Another surprising barrier is cost. The price of disposable nappies has hugely reduced in recent years and a pack of disposable nappies is actually a similar price to the same pack thirty years ago, despite inflation rates! Two young children in nappies used to take a much bigger percentage out of a family's weekly outgoings than they do today. Using the argument that getting your child out of nappies will save you loads of money doesn't have the same clout or urgency it used to.

Potty training doesn't normally happen overnight. It's a process. Most children take around six months to fully grasp this skill. Parents that are under work pressure, increasingly rely on childcare settings and schools to start the process for them.

Children have Changed

Tips for toileting.

Look out for signs that a child is ready. Common signs are spotting when a child goes to hide somewhere, like behind a sofa, when they are soiling. This is a sure sign they are aware of what's happening. If they cry because they are wet and uncomfortable, they are also beginning to recognise they need changing.

Your child may not have the words to communicate at this stage, so look out for signs in their body language. They may pull a heavy wet nappy off, or put their hand in their nappy to show you they need changing. You might notice them taking an interest in others using a potty or toilet, climbing onto the toilet themselves or pulling their nappy down.

Notice if they go for longer periods with a clean nappy as that is a sign they are holding on for longer. Give your child lots of positive attention when they do show signs of awareness, even if they just sit on a potty and don't actually produce anything.

Once you are ready to start toileting, communication between all adults involved is essential. There is no point starting training for two hours in playgroup or Nursery if it's not followed up by a childminder, grandparents or parents for the remainder of the day. Everyone needs to be on the same page.

Children have Changed

Interestingly, it's thought that when a toddler is able to jump with both feet leaving the ground, they have the physiological readiness to control the sphincter muscle that holds liquid in the bladder. This usually happens around eighteen months - much earlier than we traditionally start toilet training, but there is no reason why you can't start toileting a child of that age.

Some children use a potty, others an adapted toilet seat and some children may go straight to the toilet. There's no right or wrong way. Do what works best for you. Whichever method you choose, make it as natural as part of the day as possible. Keep a potty around and encourage them to sit on it. If you have older children, get them to model sitting on the potty or toilet.

There are some lovely picture books to reinforce positive messages about toileting. A few of my favourite are:

- o No more Nappies by Marion Cockily

- o Come out Mr Poo! By Janelle McGuinness and Jen VP

- o Liam Goes Poo in the Toilet by Jane Whalen-Banks

- o No More Nappies: A Potty Training Book. By Marion Cocklico

Children have Changed

Positive parenting

Positive praise for even having a go and lots of praise for success always works better than scolding for not trying or not producing the goods. If a child really doesn't want to do it yet, don't give up. Keep offering the potty or toilet regularly, with lots of smiles and encouragement.

I recently asked for toileting advice from an experienced medical professional who works in the preschool neurological department of our local hospital. Her surprising advice was, *don't wait for your child. Adults need to instigate toilet training as soon after eighteen months as they can and that goes for children with delayed development too*. Attitudes used to lean towards waiting until the child showed signs of being ready, but that advice has now shifted.

Advice for children with medical conditions.

Children with developmental delay may take longer than others of the same age to learn self-help skills, but almost all children can eventually learn to be clean and dry. It may seem a huge step, but it's important to start because the longer we leave it, the harder it can become. Children can become used to nappies and the habit can be a hard one to break. The earlier we start the better.

146

Children have Changed

If your child has a speech or language delay, don't let that put you off. There are plenty of other ways to communicate.

- o Try using a sign for nappy (tap two fingers on your hips) as you say the word nappy.

- o Use objects to reference a nappy change, for example hold up a nappy to indicate it's time to come to the mat.

- o Show them the potty when it's time to come and try.

- o Some children may respond better to an associated sound, like a tinkling bell sound when it's time to try.

There is no one size fits all here. Trial and error are the key, but please remember if your child has a developmental delay, it will take longer, so don't give up too soon.

A rise in infant constipation.

Health practitioners and nurseries are noticing a growing trend in Early Years children being prescribed Movicol for constipation. This may well be linked to the rise in baby gadgets like baby bouncers, where children don't get enough opportunities to

Children have Changed

develop their core muscles by spending enough time in the crawling stages.

There is also research to suggest that children who may have autistic traits are more likely to become constipated. However, you can still start toilet training. Children with ASD can often find changes and transitions difficult, so the earlier we instigate toilet training the better, so their routine isn't disrupted later. There are children who may experience sensory issues around toileting, and we will undoubtedly need to allow more time (and patience), but there is still no reason to delay.

Societal changes may be to blame for some instances of infant constipation but there are also children who have genuine medical reasons. Constipation affects up to seventy per cent of children with Down Syndrome, possibly due to slow gut transit, but whatever the underlying cause, constipation will never get better on its own and children don't just *grow out of it*. They may need laxatives for medical reasons, they may need a change in their diet and exercise, but we will need to address it.

The following website has some excellent resources to help with toilet training your child.

eric.org.uk

The Down Syndrome Association also produce excellent toileting guidance which can be helpful to

Children have Changed

support children with delayed development. (Your child doesn't have to have Down Syndrome to benefit from their advice and guidance). You can find their website by following the link below:

https://downsyndromeuk.co.uk/about-dsuk/

The duty of equality

The number of early years children that are on reduced timetables or in some extreme circumstances, excluded from school because they are not toilet trained is both hidden and alarming. Whilst I totally understand the impact a child in nappies can have on a classroom routine and the strain it places on the adult to child ratios, excluding the child and shaming the parent is not the answer.

The 2010 Equality act places a duty on us all to make reasonable adjustments in our provision for everyone, regardless of their disability. This means schools cannot turn children away because they are delayed in their development.
However, parents and teachers need to work together here. We don't need to turn children away or ask parents to come into school to change their child, but we do need to have a clear policy with responsibility on both sides.

If you have large numbers of children entering your school still in nappies or pull ups, or your children have significantly delayed self-help skills, invite your

149

Children have Changed

parents in and talk together about the benefits of developing self-help skills like toileting, using a spoon independently, dressing and undressing; whatever your children may be delayed with. Explain the burden it places on the school, the time that could be spent on more exciting, worthwhile activities and that it is to the child's benefit to be out of nappies if at all possible.

I've never met a parent yet that doesn't want the best for their child, but I've met many misinformed or uninformed parents. We need to share our knowledge here. If your parents are working and daytime meetings are difficult, you might prefer to offer an evening session or a Teams call (there are benefits to technology after all).

Explain that you want the very best for each child and that includes dignity, success, freedom, independence, less stigma, reduced cost, a positive impact on the planet - both locally as the bins won't be full of smelly nappies and globally because of the CO_2 emissions created by nappies.

Give out the data. Share the facts. It's always better to work together where children are involved, than work against each other.

Chapter 6

Supporting Schematic Behaviours

Why Do They Keep Tipping Things Up?

Children have Changed

Children have Changed

Case study: Ryan's story.

*R*yan was exactly one year old on 23rd March 2020, when the country first went into lockdown. He lives with both parents and his older brother. Four years on, Ryan prefers to play on his iPad than to play with his toys. His screen habit started young when he would cry for his Mum's phone and he quickly learned to find the app to play Candy Crush. Over the past few years, Ryan has spent long periods of time indoors, on screen, strapped into his high chair or buggy. He didn't go to a childcare setting and has not seen a health visitor since his twelve-month screening, (which he passed).

Recently, Ryan has started school. His teacher allowed him time to settle in, but she is now concerned because Ryan can't seem to sustain his attention for more than a few seconds. He wulks around the classroom tipping everything onto the floor seemingly unaware of the consequences. He also throws objects like blocks, toy cars and pencils skywards as though they are missiles. He doesn't seem to know what to do with a book; he flings them upwards too. He does like the water tray, where he scoops and tips water continually.

His play is very repetitive. He seems to do the same things over and over again. He isn't ready to take part in pretend play and he often seems oblivious to the

Children have Changed

other children. Outdoors, Ryan is unsure of himself and walks the perimeter of the fence on a continuous loop

What's going on with children's play?

Ryan is typical of many children entering our schools with delayed development. He has missed out on early opportunities to play, interact and explore and is stuck in an earlier stage of play than we are used to seeing in school. (More on Ryan later).

Children learn in lots of different ways. They learn by doing things, by having first-hand experiences and by using all their senses. They learn by having hands-on opportunities and by exploring real-life authentic resources. They learn by talking and listening and copying one another, trying things out, by getting it wrong, and by having opportunities to repeat things. Repetition is such a key factor in young children's learning.

But teachers are noticing something fundamental has changed about children's play skills. Normally, children who enter school are ready to start pretending. You can picture the scene in the home corner; children role playing pouring themselves an imaginary cup of tea and shaking the frying pan to cook the obligatory plastic fried egg. They'll wrap up the doll and rock it to sleep in the toy pram or push toy cars along a make-believe road, making *brrmm* noise. They'll pretend to

Children have Changed

bake cakes outdoors in the mud kitchen, or pretend to be their superhero (mummy, daddy or teacher usually) all the time chatting about what they are doing.

When children start school, the solitary stage of play, where children are not yet interested or aware of other children, has usually passed. Typically, children begin school around the time they are entering the parallel stage of play (standing next to another child, observing, but not always talking or interacting with them) and are starting to move into the associative and cooperative stages of play.

Instead, an increasing number of children are lagging behind. Imaginative and pretend play are not yet emerging and so interactions between children are less likely. I visited a Nursery classroom recently and couldn't put my finger on what was wrong until it suddenly hit me! None of the children were talking to each other. The classroom, although busy, and full of activity, was strangely silent. None of the children had reached the interactive stage of play. This is concerning.

Instead, the play we are seeing in school age is more akin to the typical stages of a young toddler. Classrooms are suddenly full of unwanted, and repetitive behaviours such as:

- o Tipping up trays or boxes of resources and moving on.

Children have Changed

o   Throwing, casting or launching objects.

o   Children squeezing themselves into small, inappropriate spaces.

o   Spinning themselves around until they are dizzy or spinning items with fascination.

o   Posting objects into inappropriate places.

o   Carelessly dropping objects to the floor with seemingly no awareness.

Why are they doing this?

The above examples can be categorised as schematic behaviours and they are typical examples of how younger children play, before they progress to more sophisticated stages of play like imaginative play. If you've never heard of schematic behaviours before, please don't worry. You are not alone. It's rarely mentioned in teacher training and I'm ashamed to say in my early career, I taught Nursery for years, never having heard of them. Child development doesn't seem to feature very highly in schools that are full of …. what are they called again? Oh yes…. children!

Again, Again - Understanding Schemas in Young Children by Stella Louis, Clare Beswick, Liz Marrow and Lisa Hayes is the best book I have found as an

Children have Changed

introduction to schemas. I recommend it as a good starting point. In the book, schemas are described as:

Patterns of repeated behaviour which children use to explore and express their developing ideas and thoughts through play and exploration.

How we learn.

One of the best ways to learn anything new is through repetition. If you are learning to play an instrument, unless you are a musical genius, you have to practice. Practice means repeating. After a few tries, you may manage to play a couple of notes in the right order, but you have to keep going back, trying again and again, before the notes stick in your head and your fingers grasp a kind of muscle memory. Then you move onto the next phrase of music, knowing you've really got it.

It's the same with anything. If you are learning to drive, you can't just jump in the car and go. You have to practice the movements of the pedals and gears, you need someone at the side of you, reminding you of the moves. A lot of practice lessons have to happen before you're confident enough to drive independently. The same applies to swimming, or riding a bike. All of these skills have to be repeated until we're so familiar with the movements, we can do them automatically.

Young children are no different. They need to practice and repeat. They need to revisit skills and concepts many times before they grasp new learning.

Children have Changed

That repetition is essential to help their brain make new connections. Only through regular opportunities for repetition can children learn a new skill, consolidate it, reinforce it and secure it, so that it is in their brain to be retrieved whenever they need it.

Brain development made simple.

A newborn baby's brain looks quite different to the image we usually associate with a brain. You know what I mean, that lumpy grey mass of squiggly wormlike sections. But a prenatal and newborn's brain is actually much smoother and looks something more akin to a chicken breast fillet. It's only when babies begin to repeat and practice actions, start to move their little bodies and process new language, that their brain gradually changes shape and starts to develop into the more typical representation we know of as our grey matter.

But a newborn's brain isn't completely empty. Imagine a smooth (chicken fillet) brain full of neurones, all fired up and flashing away searching for a connection with another neurone, but unable to move to reach it. That's where repetition comes in. Each time a pattern of behaviour is repeated, the connecting pathway between one neurone gets closer to a partner neurone. The more opportunities a child has to practice repeated patterns of behaviour, the more connections they are able to make. (Like a join the dots puzzle for the brain.)

Children have Changed

Do you remember learning to ride a bike? Each time you got on the bike, the connection between the two "bike riding neurones" in your brain lit up. The feeling of your foot on the peddle started to become familiar and the connection between the neurones strengthened. That feeling of holding on tight and turning the handlebars in the direction you want to go started to feel easier, more natural, and the communication along the neurone pathway became faster and faster. Then, after many tries and wobbles, on the right sized bike, with the right help and the right weather, you finally grasped peddling a two-wheeler.

Cracked it! *Wheeee…* Your neurone pathway fused itself. You hard-wired your brain and the bike riding skill will be with you for the rest of your life. You'll never forget it because that now ultra speedy connection of electrical impulses became coated in a protective layer of fat called a myelin sheath, meaning that whenever we need that connection it is there in its insulated pathway.

The importance of physical movement

It's worth mentioning that the *physical* repetitions we go through to learn to ride a bike or swim or play an instrument, play a crucial factor in helping the brain to hard wire each connection. Physical activity is fundamental to child development so we must allow children time for physical movement as they are

Children have Changed

learning. Those movements literally help the brain to make new connections and wire itself. If we try to stop children moving, and sit them at tables too soon, we are actually inhibiting brain development, rather than promoting it.

As babies grow into toddlers, they learn to gain control over their movements and an amazing process starts to take place. Tentative neural pathways are flashing away in their brains, like beacons in the dark, looking for other beacons. By repeating patterns of behaviour over and over, children are strengthening those pathways. In the Early Years, play is the best and most valuable vehicle for this to happen.

Play.

Sometimes, people can be a bit dismissive of play. It's a word we think of as a bit frivolous, something you do when you've finished your work. Go and play, we often hear, or they're just playing, but play is essential to brain development. It's a serious business.

As the clinical psychologist and author Kay Redfield Jamison says:

"Children need the freedom and time to play. Play is not a luxury. Play is a necessity."

We have a tendency to think of play as a time when you use your imagination to pretend to be someone else or take part in role play, like the examples at the

Children have Changed

beginning of this chapter. We can be guilty of assuming that play only really happens in areas like the home corner, the mud kitchen or the road-mat with the toy cars. Imaginative play is certainly important, but play doesn't always look like that.

Every child plays, but play can look very different, depending on the stage the child is at. Babies and toddlers are not always ready to make the leap of pretending to be someone else yet. They haven't got the understanding to pretend that objects can represent something else (like singing into a hairbrush to represent a microphone). Babies and toddlers play in a more repetitive way. They are testing out notions and concepts, trying things out again and again, to see if the same thing always happens.

The beginnings of play

We sometimes forget, that as adults, we have already processed many concepts that we now take completely for granted. Take gravity, for example. Without even thinking about it, we know what will happen when we drop something. Of course we do. Long ago, in our early childhood, we dropped items repeatedly. We dropped our spoon when we were in a high chair and wondered what had happened to it. Our parents handed it back to us, only for us to drop it again to test out the theory that it would once again … fall. *How amazing!*

We picked up sticks or stones outside and then let go, so they fell to the ground. We dropped toys out of our

Children have Changed

pushchair, played with balls and beanbags and bubbles, watching them fall in a downwards direction. We probably drove our poor parents a bit mad, but through those early experiences, we learned that what goes up must come down and we gradually processed the concept of gravity, meaning we no longer felt the need to test it out with every possible missile in our grasp.

The same thing happened with object permanence. As adults, we take it for granted that just because we can no longer see an object, it still exists. We've forgotten how we once believed that an object ceased to exist, once it was out of sight. If we were fortunate, we had attentive parents who played peek a boo games, hid items under cloths and made them magically appear again. When we could crawl, we probably opened kitchen cupboards to see what was behind the doors, we may have been fascinated with how rubbish seemingly disappeared into a bin. Gradually we came to an understanding and acceptance that when things were put away, out of our sight, they hadn't disappeared in a magical puff of smoke. All of our early experiences added up and eventually, object permanence became hard wired into our brains.

But here's the kicker. We were granted those opportunities and experiences. There are many children who have not been so lucky and their lack of opportunities to play means they are stuck in an earlier developmental phase. Then there are other children

Children have Changed

who may have a neurological condition that means they have a lot more difficulty in processing new concepts. Those children are going to take longer to work out how planet Earth works, and we need to be patient as they try to make sense of concepts that we as adults take for granted.

Adjusting our expectations.

These repeated patterns of behaviour (schemas) are perfectly acceptable in babies and toddlers. We expect them to drop objects to the floor, to post cake into the DVD player or turn taps on as they try to understand how rotation works. Babies and toddlers are finding their bearings, learning how their body takes up space in relation to other objects in their world. This is their play. It's cute, endearing, often amusing and we simply accept it.

It's quite normal to see babies and toddlers tipping, throwing, posting, transporting objects, lining up and positioning objects. They are working out how things work. Repeated patterns of behaviour or schematic behaviour is a good sign. Frustrating as this can sometimes be for adults, it means they are exploring. They are investigating. Their neurone beacons are calling to one another. They need time to practice and repeat. They need to seriously play. This is what children like Ryan are doing. He is not being naughty. He is trying to make sense of his world.

Children have Changed

Understanding unwanted behaviours.

You and I both know what a box of Duplo looks like when it is neatly stored away in a box, we also both know what that same box would look like if we were to tip that box up, spilling the contents all over the floor. We take it for granted. But let's remember, children like Ryan might not yet know the outcome of tipping. The exciting *sshhhhiiisshhh* tipping noise, the physical action of turning over the box, the exciting constellations the toys spill out into, once they are splayed across the floor and into the corners, the way the box is now suddenly full of empty space. This is all so fascinating it causes a child's brain to light up and call to partner neurones. (Even as it causes us to throw our hands up in despair).

The older children get, the more out of whack this behaviour seems, but at the moment, teachers are seeing these kinds of repetitive behaviours later and later. Twenty years ago, most people didn't know about schemas. We stifled this kind of play in favour of adult led tasks. We sat young children around tables too soon and asked them to follow our lead. How I wish I could go back in time with the knowledge of schemas that has been shared with the world since then. Thankfully, we are beginning to understand that young children repeat actions because they need to. They are not trying to torment us. If we keep preventing these behaviours, children simply won't be able to move on.

Children have Changed

Considerations for Pandemic babies.

Consider the challenges of the past few years. Parents who were trying to work from home, used screens as babysitters and strapped children into high chairs, buggies, baby walkers, cots or bouncers to contain them as best they could. This is not to judge parents. We were all trapped. Playgrounds lay empty, mother and toddler groups were closed, Jungle Jim's and Play Barns deserted. Grand-parents houses and gardens were off limits. Opportunities for toddlers to freely throw objects up to see if they fell down, post objects to see if they really disappeared, spin objects and line up objects to see how they looked were curtailed for some babies and toddlers.

Babies today may own more material possessions than previous generations, but they also have fewer opportunities to freely move around, due to the increase in baby "gadgets" for transportation. Gadgets like high chairs, car seats, buggies, bouncers, walkers and travel cots. Opportunities to physically move to help bond those neural pathways are becoming increasingly limited, often due to societal pressures, like parents having to get to work on time.

What can we do to overcome this?

Our challenge is to respond, adapt and provide resources and experiences that help children to move through these stages of play at their own pace. If we

165

Children have Changed

don't, we run the risk of not providing an inclusive environment.

Recently, I asked a large group of Nursery and Reception teachers how many of them made observations of schematic behaviour in their classroom. Only a tiny percentage had even heard of schemas. This is not the fault of hard-working teachers, pressed for time, and often working under top-down pressure to get children ready to read and write. (That's not to say we shouldn't encourage children to read and write; of course we should), but first we must make sure children are at an appropriate stage in their development to be able to cope with it or we are wasting our time and theirs.

My teacher training didn't fully equip me to understand child development. Over thirty years later, many newly-qualified teachers still lack a basic knowledge and understanding of child development in practice (not just the theory). There have been some great attempts to include this information into a system-wide approach, like the Solihull training model, where everyone in the area that comes into contact with children are trained in child development. More recently, Trauma Informed Schools training programs are equipping schools with a deeper understanding of child development, but there are still plenty us of that don't understand what children are communicating through their behaviour.

Children have Changed

Understanding child development is the key to good teaching. If we understand what children are doing when we observe, and more importantly, why they are doing it, we can provide the most appropriate experiences to help our children learn and grow.

Changes in development.

Just over twenty years ago, many children did enter school more able to sit and learn, because they had different experiences to todays 'children.

- o Less screen time.
- o More outdoor time.
- o More free time spent on their tummies to crawl and roll, pull up and explore.
- o Less time being transported in baby "gadgets."
- o More time spent with extended family.
- o Less temptation of fast-food
- o Less disruption to sleep patterns

But things have changed. Our children have changed. Today, they are entering schools with a different wiring system in their brains. We need to adapt if we are going to meet their needs.

Common schema.

There are multiple types of schemas. Sometimes a child will have a very strong, predominant schema that

Children have Changed

they become engrossed in, repeating it again and again. Other children may have more than one schema going on at the same time. Schemas typically change and morph into other more complex schemas as children get older.

The eight most common groups of schematic behaviour that you are most likely to see in young children are described below:

Transporting.

Children in the transporting schema have a need to move objects from one place to another because they are exploring the process of transportation. They may have been transported themselves in cars, buggies, or in their parent's arms and they are exploring the way it feels to do so. Look out for children who fill up the toy pram with random objects and then transport them to seemingly random corners of the room. They may fill their own pockets with small objects. Don't jump to conclusions here – they are probably just transporting objects. They may find small random objects and hoard them in corners or secret hiding places.

To support them, offer: ways of transporting such as prams, wheelbarrows, trucks, trugs, bikes with trailers, and other ways of carrying objects like: shopping bags, handbags, string bags, baskets, bowls, purses, rucksacks, transporter toys, toy baby slings.

Children have Changed

Positioning

Children in the positioning schema will have the need to position objects in certain ways such as lining objects up. They are learning to make sense of their own position in the world and how other objects fit in relation to themselves. To put it simply, things look different in different places and they are testing this out to check that it's true. You may spot children putting toys in long rows or lines. They might play with their food and move it around their plate, perhaps refusing to place certain foods next to other foods, or even on the same plate. They may lie on the floor next to things, lie on top of the dog, line up all the shoes in order of size, or tell other children to line up or stand in a particular place.

To support them you can provide: Blocks, construction toys, cars, dolls of various sizes, placemats and utensils to set the table, natural materials like pebbles, stones, conkers, sticks, for ordering and lining up. Be careful not to jump to the conclusion that lining up toys means your child has Autism – many children line up toys as part of their natural development as they try to make sense of their world.

Enveloping

Children who are in the enveloping schema are exploring the concept that objects, including people, can be completely enveloped. They may remember the

169

Children have Changed

feeling of being swaddled and want to repeat it. They may have a need to cover something, like swaddling a doll or wrapping themselves up in a blanket. You may spot them wrapping random objects in blankets, towels or tea-towels. They may like to get into a box and close the lid. Some children will enjoy being in dens or hideouts or will squeeze themselves into small places, like hiding in the curtains or burrowing under the covers. Maybe they push their food all over their plate until it is completely concealed or paint all over the paper until you can't see any paper at all.

To support these children, provide: large pieces of fabric, den building materials like tarpaulins or blankets, small enclosed spaces, tunnels, wrapping paper.

Enclosure

Children in the enclosure schema often build walls or structures that shut things inside because they are learning that you can enclose something or you can be enclosed yourself. They will often be spotted building walls around things like farm animals. They might close themselves in with their toys, build walls with pillows or teddys, draw borders around their paintings or pictures, or even push all their food to the edges of their plate to make a space in the middle.

To support these children, offer: farm or zoo toys with lots of fences, good quality block play, large

Children have Changed

rubber bricks to build larger enclosures, cushions, pillows, tarpaulins and dens.

Rotational

Children in the rotational schema have a need to turn or spin objects as they are trying to make sense of the fact that objects, including themselves can rotate. Remember, up to this point, they may only have realised you can travel forward and backwards or rock from side to side. Spinning is a new sensation. It's easy to forget how fascinating this is. They may rotate objects such as spinning the wheels of a toy car or perhaps turn taps on, with no particular interest in the water. They may have a fascination with spinning themselves around, sometimes until they fall over dizzy, or they might ask you to repeatedly spin them around.

To support these children, offer: toys with wheels, windmills, toy globes, hoola-hoops, construction toys with rotary blades and wheels and any other opportunities to rotate objects in a safe way.

Connecting

Children in the connecting schema have a fascination with joining objects together and will have an interest in connecting things that can be stuck together or pulled apart. They may be fascinated with the Velcro on shoes, constantly opening and closing it, or they

Children have Changed

may repeatedly join pieces of Duplo or connecting toys together, without attempting to build anything.

To support these children, offer: zips, buttons, Velcro, laces, bows, string, Sellotape, glue, construction toys, Stickle-bricks, Lego, Duplo, magnetic blocks, jigsaws, connecting beads on a string / thread pasta on string necklaces, or tear and share brioche buns.

Orientation

Linked to all the above schemas, children in the orientation schema are developing an awareness of space, how they fit into it and how things can be positioned around them. They are literally trying to orientate themselves in relation to their surroundings. Asking these children to sit for prolonged time is the opposite of what they physically and intellectually need. You may spot children lying down against other objects, rolling down slopes, or exploring the world at different levels.

To support these children, offer: large spaces, tunnels, ramps, slopes, slides, climbing frames, trees and bushes to climb.

Trajectory

Children in a trajectory schema are trying to make sense of the way objects can move and how we can track objects with our eyes. They are also learning to

Children have Changed

grasp and release their grip to drop and squeeze objects. You may spot them lying down and looking at the ceiling, tipping back on the sofa to see the world upside down, bending down and looking between their legs, or they may look intently along lines of railings, or bannisters. Some children may climb inappropriate places, roll around, or ask you to turn them upside down.

To support these children, offer: buckets and balls to practice posting, tipping them out and retrieving them. Soft balls and beanbags can be a great way of exploring tipping and posting in a safe and fun way.

The building blocks for life

Understanding these stages is essential in today's classrooms. We are only recently beginning to realise how many children are still progressing through these stages as they enter school. So, if you see a child, like Ryan, tipping things up or knocking things over, repeatedly pouring water or becoming fascinated with turning the taps on, throwing objects upwards or posting objects into small holes, try to remember that child is in the throes of schematic behaviour and is only trying to make sense of his world.

Adapting our practice to support them can be challenging and out of our comfort zone but we need to change if we are going to meet these children's needs. Parents and practitioners all need to understand

Children have Changed

what is happening and how we must change to support our children's development.

A true story.

Back in the day, as a frazzled, young mum, I had no idea what these repetitive behaviours meant. One of my daughters used to post objects repeatedly as a toddler. She posted slices of toast and jam into our DVD player, coins and small stones went into wellingtons and shoes. She posted a paper straw into the gas fire, nearly setting the house of fire and she posted her sister's shoes into the fish tank. When she found her dad's wage packet, full of twenty-pound notes (this was nearly thirty years ago) she posted them out all of our front door letterbox into the wind. If only I'd know about schemas!!

Setting boundaries:

This is not about giving in to a child's every whim. There is a wealth of ways to support schematic play, but it's still important to set boundaries. As children get older and larger, throwing, tipping or posting objects becomes a lot more problematic. Decide on what you allow in your setting (or home) and stick to it. All the adults need to be saying the same thing so that you have a consistent approach. Schematic behaviours need to be talked about and reviewed regularly so everyone knows where the children are in their learning journey.

Children have Changed

If you have children at the casting stage, they will need opportunities to throw in a safe way but you might decide to remove heavy or dangerous "missiles" like large pebbles or wooden blocks. Alternatively, you may decide to use it as a teachable moment and stop the children throwing indoors with a clear command and signal. Instead of trying to deal with flying missiles indoors - go outdoors and provide bubbles, bean bags, soft balls or balloons.

If you have children who turn on the taps because they are fascinated with things that rotate, give a clear signal that it's not acceptable to leave the taps running because it wastes water and can cause flooding. Instead, provide different opportunities like spinning tops or fidget spinners.

How to move forward:

- o Hold information sessions for parents/ carers on schematic play. Teachers who work with older children would also benefit from knowing about schemas as some children are still presenting with these behaviours further up the school.

- o Regularly observe the children in your care for evidence of intense interests and then provide safe ways to support it.

Children have Changed

- o Talk to governors, senior leaders and parents about early child development and how to best support it. They need to understand where the children are at and why you are changing your practice.

- o Set clear boundaries and expectations in your setting, but also provide safe and appropriate opportunities for children to follow their own interests.

- o Find out more about schemas – you need only Google - there is a wealth of information on the internet to help you support children.

- o Remember that there is a reason behind every behaviour. Some unwanted behaviours are only a child's need to understand or make sense of their world. If we keep providing the same things we have always done, we run the risk of not meeting these children's needs and their delay will be further prolonged.

Children have Changed

Chapter 7.

How to Support Children with Delayed Motor Skills.

I'm Having to Feed Them at Snack Time!

Children have Changed

Children have Changed

Case Study: Stanley's story.

I *first met Stanley when he was approaching three years old. His health visitor had referred him to our outreach team, as he'd noticed Stanley had failed to meet several of his expected milestones. I went to meet him in his childcare setting and found a bundle of giggling energy with a mass of curls sitting on the floor in his designer tracksuit.*

Stanley could only be described as floppy. He didn't seem to have the muscle tone to support his bones. He could walk, but after a few steps would flop to the floor like a rag doll. His balance and coordination were also poor and at lunch time I noticed how he struggled to manipulate a spoon to his mouth without his yoghurt flicking in all directions. He also protested loudly at any kind of messy play like play dough, sand or gloop and seemed averse to touching any new textures. He was delayed in quite a few areas of learning, but since he'd started in a childcare setting, he had started to make considerable progress.

I spoke to Stanley's mum at length, and found out that the family had experienced a hard lockdown. They'd had had no contact with the outside world for months. Stanley is an only child and had spent long periods of each lockdown in his baby bouncer or car seat.

"He loved his bouncer," his mum told me. "We fed him in it, he even went to sleep in it."

Children have Changed

"Right. Did Stanley ever crawl?" I asked.
"No, not much. He was late to walk. He finally walked at nineteen months."

"Did he crawl at all, before he walked?"

"Hmm, a little. Not really."

The crawling stage and why it's important.

I explained to Stanley's mum that missing out on the crawling stage can have a big impact on our brain development and our sensory perception. Crawling across different surfaces allows the brain to process information about different sensory textures like carpet, wood, grass and concrete; experiences we often take for granted as adults.

To crawl successfully, you need to move your opposite knee to your opposite hand and this requires the right and left sides of the brain to communicate with each other. Communication between the two sides of our brain is essential for all sorts of physical coordination activities in life such as walking, running and riding a bike.

Children who miss out on the crawling stage sometimes experience physical delay later. They can find it harder to hold a pencil, or like Stanley, get a spoon to their mouth. If the crawling stage has been missed altogether, it's a good idea to go back and

Children have Changed

revisit it. Even if a child is now walking, activities to encourage crawling, like pretending to be an animal, can still be used in play.

This is exactly what had happened to Stanley. He'd been physically contained for long periods in his bouncer and car seat and had missed out on opportunities to develop his core strength, coordination and balance. He was also behind with his sensory processing skills as he hadn't had sufficient opportunities to touch the floor with his hands and feet. Stanley is an extreme case. As a result of his containment, today he needs physiotherapy to support his physical development but he is making good progress. His childcare setting supports him by providing tunnels, bridges, slopes and slides, and they encourage him to crawl on a daily basis.

Babies need daily opportunities to crawl. Sometimes, well-meaning parents can try to skip this stage and encourage their child to walk before they have had enough time to fully process the crawling stage. I may well have been one of those overly competitive parents (sorry girls!) It's only now, I understand why missing out on the crawling stage is a red flag in child development, because the very act of physically crawling allows vital brain connections to be made.

The importance of physical movement.

A few years ago, I was lucky enough to attend a training event in Cardiff, where a lady called Nalda Wainwright gave a talk on the Physical Literacy

Children have Changed

project. This was an eye-opening lesson to me. She talked about recent changes in UK society, that have led to children having less opportunities to use their physical skills, including less time to roll, crawl, toddle and run.

She referred to a kind of societal slide towards a *coffee shop culture*, where children spend less time in parks, or playing outside, and instead spend more time in buggies or prams as their parents meet up at the local coffee shop. Coffee shops are a burgeoning market in the UK. She told us how many parks are now under used. Now I'm the last person to criticise a coffee break and a chat, but all of a sudden, as I walked through my local city, I started to notice how true this was. Parks were empty. Coffee shops were full. The balance of time spent on physical activity did seem to have shifted.

Constipation caused by containment.

Nalda mentioned other barriers to children having opportunities for physical play, like baby-walkers, baby-bouncers, high chairs and other gadgets that physically contained children. Once again, modern life was impacting negatively on our youngest children. Babies didn't seem to have as many opportunities to freely crawl and explore as they used to, and in losing those opportunities, they'd started to lose some of their core strength.

Children have Changed

Coincidently, there was also a reported rise in laxative medication in the Early Years. In other words, if children haven't had opportunities to develop their core muscles by crawling or pulling themselves up, and they have inactive lifestyles or if they are not in upright positions often enough, where gravity can work naturally on the body, they can become constipated.

This was horrifying! Our children were on medication usually reserved for old people who struggled to be active due to their advancing years. How could this be happening to our toddlers? Why aren't doctors prescribing tummy time, crawling and physical outdoor activities instead of medication? Fresh air, natural light and physical exercise, all promote good sleep, which in turn promotes a healthier appetite which promotes a healthy, regular system - the links were like a paper chain. Obvious but fragile.

Considerations for pandemic children.

Do you remember during lockdowns, how key workers could use childcare facilities, but they were closed off to everyone else? For a while, childcare settings and schools were like ghost towns with only children of a few chosen professions (NHS workers and delivery drivers for example) allowed in. The implication being, many children missed out on opportunities for outdoor play, time with wheeled toys, chances to roll down ramps and slopes, to slide

Children have Changed

and climb up climbing frames, to run freely and chase each other, hop skip and jump and dance, as only young children can.

If you worked in an Early Years setting at the time, you will know that there were some very stringent rules around what we were allowed to provide for children. Risk assessments forbade the use of play dough, sand play, water play, messy sensory play and cookery due to the risk of transmitting infection. Soft play was also banned. Cushions, mats and soft toys like puppets and teddies were all removed due to the potential risk of infection spreading. Provision was stripped back to the bare minimum until we knew more about the Covid 19 variant.

Quite obviously, this was to keep everyone safe, but the unintended consequences of these rules, meant that even if your child was lucky enough to be able to attend a setting, they had limited opportunities to develop their physical skills.

Pushing, pulling, rolling and stretching dough is a key factor in developing children's fine motor control. N.A.S.A.'s astronauts actually use play dough to build up the dexterity in their fingers so they can manipulate objects wearing bulky heatproof space gloves. Manipulating, digging and moulding sand; ditto.

These are the building blocks through which children develop the forty muscles from their shoulder to their fingertips so that when it is time to start to write, their

Children have Changed

muscles are strong enough to hold a pen. Without these foundations in early years, writing can be a very uncomfortable process and one that children soon become reluctant to take part in. We are sometimes accused of *just playing* in Early Years, but we are playing with purpose and for good reason. We are setting children up for success. Early Years practitioners are fantastic at this.

Messy play like shaving foam, gloop, cornflower, rainbow rice and jelly are brilliant fun, but more importantly, they are key to children developing a sensory tolerance to different textures, temperatures and wet and dry substances. They are also an exciting way for children to learn new adjectives like wet, squishy, squashy and sticky which helps broaden their vocabulary.

Children learn to make marks in messy play, setting the foundation for understanding why we write to communicate. Squeezing and squashing those substances builds up dexterity in their fingers and wrists and all of this is done in such a playful way that children have no clue that they are learning. Hands-on learning helps children experience for themselves how the world works in real life and allows them to process all those physical sensations and concepts. Pandemic restrictions put a stop to this and so today's children need more time to revisit messy play so that they have firm foundations to build on.

Children have Changed

Children with Physical delay.

I would never have predicted the number of children experiencing physical delay after the pandemic, but recent referrals to core services are evidencing an alarming rate of referrals for delayed motor skills. Teachers are noticing how children are more clumsy, uncoordinated, not as able to climb, peddle, kick a ball or are able to jump leaving the ground without adult support. (Remember that being able to leave the ground with two feet is an indicator that you have control over your sphincter muscle and are ready to control your bladder). An increasing number of children travel to school in car seats or buggies and many are coincidently, still in nappies.

"Movement is an integral part of life from the moment
of conception until death, and a child's experience
of movement will play a pivotal part in shaping his personality, his feelings, and his achievements.....
Learning is not just about reading, writing, and maths. These are higher abilities that are built upon the integrity of the relationship between brain and body."

(Goddard-Blythe, S. (2005). The Well-Balanced Child. Stroud: Hawthorn Press)

Children have Changed

Five less years.

Today's lifestyles are severely impacting our children's future life expectancy. As I mentioned at the beginning of this book, according to the UK Office for National Statistics, today's children will live on average, *five less* years than their own parents and there are other studies that are less conservative. If we don't make drastic changes, those five extra years will be lost to them forever.

How are we allowing this to happen? Why the hell isn't this talked about more?

There is a YouTube video that asks a group of children what they would do if they had five extra years. Follow the video link below to view this stark reminder: (You made need tissues).

https://www.google.com/search?client=safari&rls=en&q=PHYSICAL+LITERACY+GIVE+ME+BACK+5+YEARS&ie=UTF-8&oe=UTF-8#fpstate=ive&vld=cid:72f7a4e5,vid:BmOlzRQTabA,st:0

Children have Changed

Tips to mitigate Physical delay.

At home:

- o Wherever possible, walk. Walk to your child to the local shop, walk them to the park, walk them to school. You might not be able to do this every day, but whenever you can, do it.

- o Remember the saying "There's no such thing as bad weather, only the wrong clothes." Get outside in the fresh air, preferably into green spaces, whenever you can.

- o Don't be afraid of rough and tumble play. Pretend to be horses, and let your child ride on your back, throw them up in the air, swing them around (within reason). It's great physical exercise and builds trust between you and your child and it also help them gain a sense of their body in relation to space, gravity and angles.

- o Limit sedentary screen time wherever you can. Instead use it to find ways to incorporate and encourage movement like the Just Dance game or put on a Joe Wicks work-out with your child.

- o Don't be afraid to let your child take safe risks – Only by allowing children opportunities to climb up will they learn to moderate their own

Children have Changed

behaviour and climb back down safely. Let them climb a tree, but stand nearby in case they get stuck. Remember the benefits, as well as the risks.

○ If your child did miss out on the crawling stage, provide lots of playful ways to practise crawling – pretend to be horses racing, or farm animals or make dens that you have to crawl into.

In school / childcare:

○ Provide plenty of activities to develop children's motor control. Threading, pegging, making large circles with ribbon sticks, "painting" the walls with brushes and water, using dough, clay and pastry all help to develop the muscles in children's shoulders, arms and fingers. (most childcare settings are already fabulous at this).

○ Strengthening these muscles is essential for developing a comfortable pincer grip (the correct grip to hold a writing implement). If you are challenged as to why you are providing this, explain that there is no point in starting to write without first developing these muscles. It's too uncomfortable and it is counterproductive as it only creates reluctant writers.

Children have Changed

- o In your outdoor area, provide a digging area. This can be sand or mud, but it does need to have some depth. Digging is great for developing the core muscles and the shoulder girdle. Children love to dig for a real purpose so bury some 'treasure' and get to work.

- o Think about different surfaces, different levels and different challenges for children to navigate outdoors. Rolling down mounds, navigating steps, lifting crates or heavier loose parts, space to freely run all help to build children's physical core strength and should be happening regularly.

Parents and Teachers:

Use the Physical Literacy resources on the website below:
https://activeforlife.com/activities-for-babies-and-toddlers/

Children have Changed

Chapter 8

How to Support Sensory Behaviours

Did They Really Just Lick the Window?

Children have Changed

Children have Changed

Case Study: Zophia's Story

*Z*ophia is four years old. She is tall for her age, physically strong with a long ponytail down her back, a beautiful, shy smile and the longest eyelashes you've ever seen. Zophia has started school but struggles with many aspects of it.

She has a very short attention span and isn't ready to join in with group work. It's difficult to distract her when she is playing with something that she has chosen herself. She doesn't like to share. She can become quite distressed when the teacher shakes the tambourine to signal that it's time for snack, or time to go outside and she flat out refuses to wash her hands in school or go near the water tray.

Her parents are worried about Zophia's limited diet and their GP has recently referred them to children's health services. Despite being offered a range of food, Zophia is rigid about only eating dry textures. She has been prescribed vitamin drops but it's a daily battle for her parents to get her to take them. In school, Zophia's teacher has noticed that she sometimes has a seemingly uncontrollable urge to put objects in her mouth. She finds tiny stones in the playground and tries to crunch on them, she chews on pencils, and she has even gnawed some of the wooden blocks on the carpet.

Zophia's blood test found that she has a low iron count. Her paediatrician explained that this may

Children have Changed

account for some of the urges Zophia has to eat inappropriate objects. A course of iron supplements has helped a little, but Zophia still finds certain food textures very difficult to cope with. She pushes food away, refuses to sit and can become very distressed around meals at home and in school. Zophia has significant difficulties with sensory processing.

An Increase in Sensory Behaviours.

We're all sensitive in different ways and to different things. Some people prefer to be hot; others would choose to be cold. You may love the feel of a cosy fleece, others may shrink from it. Some people prefer spicy food, others like sweet tastes. Children are no different of course, and they all have individual preferences, but over the past few years, we have suddenly had an explosion of children presenting with sensory behaviours that are so severe, that like Zophia, they are getting in the way of their learning.

A well-developed sensory system is essential for children to become successful learners, but for some, sensory processing doesn't develop as efficiently as it should and can affect children's daily lives, learning outcomes, and social interactions. It can also be very confusing for the child, their parents and their teachers.

Common sensory behaviours I've seen recently include:

Children have Changed

- children who avoid any kind of human touch and dislike hugs.

- children who crave touch and constantly seek to feel an adult's hand or face.

- Children who are irritated by certain fabrics or clothing tags and strip off their clothes.

- Children who won't remove their jumpers, even on a blisteringly hot day.

- Children who won't wear a coat, even in the snow.

- Children who fear and won't touch wet substances such as water, wet sand, clay or jelly.

- Children who seek out being soaked, pouring water over themselves until they are drenched.

- Children who won't keep their shoes and socks on.

- Children who dislike walking on certain surfaces like grass or sand.

- Children with a heightened sensitivity to bright or flashing lights.

Children have Changed

- o Children who react with distress to certain specific sounds or loud noises.

- o Children who become stressed and anxious in crowded places, like the supermarket.

- o Children who become obsessive about mouthing objects, sucking on their sleeves until they are worn to shreds or children like Zophia who seek hard textures to gnaw or bite.

- o Children who seek sensory stimulation from sensations like licking a cold window or a rough floor surface.

This is not an exhaustive list and there are as many different sensory behaviours as there are individual children, but we are not used to seeing so many of these behaviours and at quite the intensity we are dealing with recently in school and childcare settings.

Sensory sensations

We all use our senses as a window to the world. When our brain receives messages from our senses, we process this quite subconsciously. How one person processes a sensation can be very different to another but we can all appreciate, at least to some degree, what sensory overload can feel like.

Children have Changed

For me, when someone bites on a hard boiled sweet, the crunch of their teeth as the candy splinters into shards gives me the *ick*. I can't tolerate it and have to look away and cover my ears. I can lose track of my thoughts in that moment and my reaction probably misrepresents the level of threat I'm under. (I'll probably shout something like Oh my god! Stop! and go running off). I'm sure you'll have one too. A certain sensation that makes you physically cringe. Sucking on an empty straw, perhaps? The feel of rubber gloves? The sound of nails being filed? The smell of burning plastic?

Thankfully, that boiled sweet sensation happens very rarely to me. But just imagine how it would feel to have those shuddering, cowering sensations on a regular basis, impacting on your daily routine. How difficult must it be to hold on to your emotional response at that point if your sensory input is overwhelming you? How hard must it be to think past that sensation and plan a strategy to cope with it? Especially if you are a young child, still in the early stages of language development and don't have the words to explain how you are feeling.

Depending on our earliest experiences, we all use our senses to interpret the world differently. Our responses to the world may be similar, but they are not identical. Your interpretation of certain sensations will feel different to mine. One person may associate the smell of vegetables cooking in a negative way if perhaps they had a bad experience of school dinners. Another

Children have Changed

person may love the smell of vegetables cooking because it reminds them of Sunday dinner and happy family times. The way we have developed our sensory response has been a different neurological route for us all and so our individual neural pathways are all slightly different. In other words, we all have individual quirks.

What's happening in the brain?

Children who have delayed sensory processing skills can be constantly in a state of fight or flight, as their brains struggle to process the emotional feelings caused when they experience certain sensations. Their sensory system picks up information from their surroundings and sends information to the nervous system. The nervous system processes this information and generates a response or reaction to what is happening around them.

How these sensory behaviours manifest can seem very confusing, not least because some children can seem to have contradictory sensory behaviours. They may actively seek out certain sensory experiences, like particular smells and then they may react badly to other smells.

Simple things like a label in their clothes, a certain sound, or a very particular food texture can provoke a seemingly huge over-reaction to us adults and can cause significant worry for parents. Parents who have children with severe sensory processing difficulties around food, like Zophia, can find it particularly

Children have Changed

difficult when children start to find their food distressing and confusing. These children are not being fussy. They genuinely can't tolerate the sensations associated with food.

The sensory system.

We all know about our five senses - hearing, seeing, touch, taste and smell, but we also have two less known, hidden senses that feed our brains with information about our movements and where our body is in space.

The vestibular sense sits behind our inner ear and is key to us feeling safe and well in our environment. It helps us to navigate movement, heights and gravity, for example, it lets us know we are still moving when we are standing in a lift.

The proprioceptive sense is related to our joints and muscles and it helps us understand where we arc in space, without us having to look, for example we can still reach out our hands when our eyes are closed. This sense is related to push, pull, pressure and force.

Our executive function sits in the part of the brain that controls our sensory system. In other words, our ability to plan ahead, stay focussed and exercise self-control, is controlled by our sensory system. If our senses become overwhelmed, we lose access to these functions and it can produce a similar feeling to vertigo. It can stop us in our tracks and can mean we overreact massively to seemingly insignificant things. Teachers are reporting an increase in exactly this recently. Children are reportedly flying off the handle for the slightest thing, sometimes for no clear or apparent reason at all.

This is often interpreted as attention seeking, when in actual fact, the opposite is true. Children who are able, tell us that the last thing they want to do when they feel overwhelmed is draw attention to themselves, but in that moment, they don't understand the physical sensations they are feeling and they can't explain why they suddenly need other sensory input to compensate. They may feel an urge to chew or bite down on a certain texture, to feel cold, to pull off their shoes or make a loud sound because it helps them to feel a release of pressure. They are desperately trying to regulate themselves.

Does it mean my child has autism?

Sensory processing disorders are often linked to autism, because many people on the autistic spectrum experience their sensory perception in different ways to neurotypical folk, but not everyone with sensory issues are on the spectrum. It's not a foregone conclusion. Some children experiencing significant developmental delay are still operating (in sensory terms) at the same stages a baby would and the best way to support them is to meet them at this level.

Children have Changed

How our senses develop.

All babies are sensory. Imagine the world through their eyes. Everything around them is brand new and exciting. They look towards the light, turn towards new sounds, grab at new textures, respond to familiar faces, startle easily, and become quickly overwhelmed if too much stimulation is offered.

When a baby cries, we do everything we can to try and regulate them:

- o We try changing them so they don't feel wet

- o Feeding them to regulate their hunger

- o Holding them close or rocking them so they are comforted.

- o We sing softly to them

- o We offer sensory toys like rattles, teething rings, light up toys and items they can grip tightly.

- o We blow bubbles or show them mobiles

- o We offer soft and cosy textures.

All of this sensory input helps to soothe and regulate them until they begin to develop their own executive functioning skills and control their sensory responses.

Children have Changed

If children are delayed in their development, they will still need similar opportunities to be able to soothe and regulate themselves. Every behaviour is a form of communication so if a child is having a bad reaction, they may well be struggling to process the information they have received from their senses. In this state, children will often regress right back to typical baby or toddler behaviour so we need to meet them at this level.

Considerations for Pandemic babies

We develop our sensory system through the opportunities we are granted as babies and young children. If we are allowed to take part in things like:

- o playing with food, squelching it between our fingers

- o running dry sand through our fingers

- o feeling sand between our toes at the beach

- o pouring and swirling water in the bath

- o bursting bubbles

- o Stroking the soft furry coat of a pet animal

- o Jumping in muddy puddles

Children have Changed

- ○ blowing a dandelion clock

- ○ dressing up in different fabrics

- ○ knocking wooden materials together to make sounds

…there's a very good chance our sensory system will develop.

The pandemic unfortunately put limits on these kinds of opportunities for a lot of children. It's impossible to quantify how many opportunities were missed, in the same way that we can't quantify how many facial expressions were missed due to mask wearing, but we do know that this is another area where children are experiencing delay and they need to be allowed time to catch up.

On the other hand, some children will have had many positive sensory opportunities, but may have a significant neurological delay. When children are young, we often simply don't know if they are delayed because they haven't had sufficient opportunities to develop their sensory system or if they have a neurological condition. Both scenarios can present in an almost identical way.

If you think your child may have a significant delay in sensory processing, always talk to your GP or health visitor and seek specialist advice.

Children have Changed

How to help children regulate their sensory needs:

It's not always easy to help young children regulate themselves. In fact, it's blooming hard. It can be challenging and difficult to get it right and it's very often a case of trial and error. The path to finding what works often takes time. The more honest we are when things go wrong, the more we ask for help and stay curious about our children's behaviours, the more we can learn about their sensory language. Communication between parents, teachers and caregivers is key here.

How to support children with sensory delay

We need to react to children who are distressed by sensory input as though they are at the highest level of anxiety. Always try to regulate them first. (See the advice and guidance in Chapter 2 for regulating the emotions).

- o Don't ask children questions or give them instructions when they are in distress. They won't be able to answer or understand because the brain literally can't process new information or respond to questions when it's in a dysregulated state.

- o Try to make sure that everyone in the setting has an awareness and understanding of the

204

Children have Changed

sensory system and how it may affect some children differently to others.

- o Be a sensory detective. Observe what is going on for the child, where their distress happens and their potential triggers, so we can provide (or remove) what they need to feel regulated.

- o Take a sensory tour of your environment, indoors and outdoors, with a specific child in mind and consider all their potential triggers. Consider things like bright lights, particular sounds or noises, patterns in the environment, changes in the flooring, different surfaces, textures, reflections, and shadows.

- o Notice where a child seems to feel most comfortable, safe, and secure and which areas they tend to avoid. Consider what is it about these particular areas that comfort or trigger them.

- o Provide plenty of daily opportunities for children to take part in sensory activities so children can make choices about the sensory input they need to feel regulated. Don't force children to take part. Try gently placing your hand over theirs and leading them to an activity for as long as they will tolerate, until they gain enough confidence to try it independently.

Children have Changed

○ Have a basket of figit toys to help children focus. These can be items like stress balls, small plastic figurines, a strong elastic band or a metal spoon. Some children need to hold or squeeze an object to be able to focus. These can be effective at circle time or they can also to help children drop off to sleep. It can be trial and error sometimes until you find the one that works.

○ Make sure the routine is as predictable as possible and stay calm and positive.

○ Provide a sensory space but please be cautious here. Sensory rooms or tents can look beautiful and be very aesthetically pleasing to adults, but we need to think carefully when creating them, as spaces can be over or under stimulating for individual children. If you follow the ideas above, you are more likely to get it right for the child.

○ For some children they may prefer a quiet, empty space with no stimulation to help them feel soothed and less anxious.

The Early Years pioneer Ferre Laevers tells us that for a child to have a high level of well-being they need to feel like 'a fish in water.' Sadly, many children with delayed sensory processing skills, must instead feel like a square peg in a round hole. To ease this as much

Children have Changed

as possible, we need to focus on the fact that their brains and nervous systems are still developing and go back, before we can go forward, to help them find ways of regulating and soothing their brain. Only then do they stand a chance of being able to learn. It's often helpful to reflect for a moment what the world must feel like through their eyes:

Fish out of water – An (almost) true story.

The first time I was left in the wide, tall building, with the clickerty-clack floors and smell of dead food, teacher asked my name.

"Joy," Nan said, "Her name's Joy."

I thought my name was Stoppit so I already learned a new thing. Nan said I would.

Teacher smiled down at me. "Hello Joy." I looked up. She had wheels in her ears and her face was coloured in.

"Here you go love," Nan said passing her my bag.

"What's this?" teacher asked.

"Spare nappies," Nan said.

Teacher looked disappointed. "We do prefer it if the children are toilet trained," she said.

Children have Changed

'That's all very well," said Nan, "but I work shifts and our Joy here doesn't listen."

I left them talking and ran across the big floor until I got to the patterns. Then I stepped more carefully. Up, down, over, up, down, over. The windows went up to the sky and there were climbing bars on the walls. I pulled myself up them. The stretch in my body felt lovely

"Get down! Stoppit!" Nan pulled me off the bars. Teacher's cool hand pulled me away from Nan.

"Nananananananan," I cried.

I was taken into a busy room full of big and small people. It was too hot. My eyes were wet. My feet felt wrong in the big girl black shoes. Too pinchy. They all looked at me. I hated this place. I screamed to show it. Covered my ears. Teacher crouched by me. She whispered "Nan's coming back soon," but I didn't believe her. All the nans had left their kids here. I wasn't staying. I ran for the door.

A circle shape lady with a wobbly chin caught me. She said "Shushshushshush now, stop it."

I looked at her in surprise. She knew my name. After she'd rocked and sung to me, she let me climb down. She showed me a big tray of water. She took my hand and made a splish splash with it. I liked splashing. The

Children have Changed

warm feeling made me pull at my nappy. My socks got warm. My shoes filled up. You get in the bath when you've wet. I climbed in. Two boys looked at me. They had big heads. Too much hair. One of them moved away. One shouted Stop it. I didn't like him shouting my name like that.

"Oh Joy, look at you. You're wet through," circle lady said.

"Stoppit," I tried to tell her. Don't you know my name's Stoppit?

She took me into a corner to peel off my wet clothes. I shouted for Nan as loud as I could. How could she leave me here. It was too bright. Too many colours. It smelt like clean bathrooms, bananas and Sundays. The small ones bumped into me. The walls flapped with papers. Things swung from the ceiling. It was too much. I made my humming noise. I ran up and down. Up and down, up and down to make me feel better.

"What's that dreadful noise for?" Teacher came over with her sad face on.

She sat me on a hard chair. I got up. Teacher put me back. I got up. It was too hard.

"We sit down at snack time," she said. "Here's your fruit."

Children have Changed

The plate smelled like sick. The banana was mushy. I got up. I needed to get away from the smell. I ran to the corner of the busy room. I hid in a little kitchen. Another lady tried to pull me back to the bad smells. I shouted and twisted away from her. I lay on the floor. She tried to take my hands. I hid them.

"Leave her there," Teacher said. "She can have her drink over there for today."

Circle lady brought a plastic cup with milk. I kicked her away. Why wouldn't they leave me alone? All I wanted was to go home.

I couldn't live here.

A fish out of water.

The story above is an imagined example, based on a number of real children, to help consider how children with sensory processing delay can experience a childcare setting or classroom. Despite there being plenty of well-meaning adults on hand to support Joy, she is struggling.

Try reading Joy's story again and see if you can spot all the sensory triggers.

Now use the list of ways to support sensory behaviours to see how Joy could be made to feel more comfortable in her new environment.

Children have Changed

Chapter 9

Supporting delayed Speech, Language and Communication skills.

Why aren't they talking yet?

Children have Changed

Children have Changed

The Frustration of Delayed Speech and Language.

I magine for a moment that you have lost the power of speech. You need to navigate your way through next week without being able to say a word to anyone. You can't ask questions, give instructions, make small talk or share greetings with anyone. Imagine trying to do your job, run your home or care for your family when you can't communicate with them.

If you are anything like me, you're likely to feel a great deal of frustration, annoyance, maybe even despair. Messages are likely to get lost in translation and you may, quite reasonably, feel like giving up even trying.

Now put yourself in the shoes of a child who can't yet form words and may not be able to process more than one spoken word at a time. How confusing, frustrating, irritating and defeated must it feel to be in a setting, surrounded by a language that you are locked out of? No wonder there is an increase in aggressive behaviours. Behind those unwanted behaviours is a huge unmet need. It's so *frustrating* not being able to communicate.

Alongside children with speech and language delay, there is also a steep increase in children who have delayed social communication skills. These children don't initiate interactions. They play alone. They are solitary. They don't come and ask us when they need something. They don't tell us when they want more of

213

Children have Changed

something or have had enough of something. These children also experience frustration. At first sight, they may appear to have no empathy or understanding for other children around them, but we have to remember that they are at a much earlier stage of social development than we are used to seeing in our schools. I am sadly seeing this on a daily basis.

True Story

I recently ran a training course on child development for headteachers, teachers and teaching assistants working in the early years. I began by asking what kind of challenges they were facing in their own classrooms. I knew teachers were finding it difficult, but I wasn't prepared for the outpouring of emotion that followed. The room fell deathly silent. Teachers looked nervously around the room, wondering who would speak first. One teacher bravely raised her hand.

"Yes?" I encouraged.

"There are just so many children in our school with delays," she said. "It's like the world has completely changed," she looked apologetic and emotional as she spoke.

"Yes," I agreed, "We are also working with children every day in our team. We're seeing it too."

Children have Changed

That did it. The room erupted. Teachers spoke up with passion, animation and genuine concern about their classrooms, full of children still in nappies, who couldn't feed themselves, couldn't regulate their emotions and their greatest, number one concern was that many of these children were still unable to talk.

"It's just so difficult when you want to help them but they can't communicate."

"They know how to use an iPad, but they don't respond to their own name!"

"They can't tell us when something is wrong. We have so many tears, it's not right."

"They don't respond to simple instructions, or know the names of everyday objects."

"How are we supposed to get them to read and write when they can't even talk?"

"They don't play with each other. They don't seem to even notice that other children are there."

"Why have things changed so much?"

Why indeed?

Children have Changed

The Importance of Early Speech and Language.

The concern shown by teachers around children's delayed speech, language and communication skills is equally matched by their parents. When I meet with parents, it's what they almost always wish most for their child. The ability to be able to communicate, to tell us what they want or need, to let us know their preferences, is the key to unlocking so much of the frustration that their children are experiencing. But also, the sheer joy of that moment when your child first says the word Mummy or Daddy, the first time you overhear your child having a conversation with another child or singing the refrain of a favourite song are magical moments, denied to many parents at the moment.

The importance of time.

Early Years practitioners have been banging the drum for years about the importance of children being granted time to develop oracy skills. There is no point in starting to read or write before children can hold a conversation and have something to write about. Speech, Language and Communication is the foundation for all other learning and rightly so, is now prioritised in most Foundation Stage classrooms.

Early Years classrooms have progressed massively over the last twenty years and now include plenty of experiential, hands on learning. Most settings are set up with exciting practical areas of learning rather than

Children have Changed

tables and chairs and the outdoors is used as much as the indoors to develop children's play. Time for play is vital when children are developing language because children are influenced more by other children than they are by adults. They need plenty of time to play with other children, alongside adults that understand how and when to intervene to scaffold new language. This is the key to successful language development but this all takes time.

Why speech, language and communication matter.

As well as feeling a lot less frustration, children who develop decipherable speech and a good understanding and comprehension of the language pattens and conventions we use, are at an immediate advantage in every area of the curriculum.

- They can follow simple instructions which means they can follow the classroom routine.

- They find it easier to build friendships which means their emotional wellbeing is higher.

- They can ask when they need help, and explain when something is wrong.

- They experience far fewer misunderstandings.

Children have Changed

- o They can express their feelings so have fewer anxieties and upsets.

There is absolutely no point starting to learn phonic sounds, copy out letters or learn to write numbers if a child hasn't grasped the basics of speech. Yet, I've still seen this happen, time and time again.

The current UK picture.

There is plenty of evidence that the UK is falling further and further behind in supporting children's Speech, Language and Communication skills. On 04 September 2023, Speech and Language UK published a report that found a staggering number of children with speech and language challenges had been recorded. Shockingly, at least 1.9 million school aged children are now estimated to be behind in long term Speech, Language and Communication needs (SLCN) including talking and understanding the meaning of words. A new report from the charity, listening to Unheard Children agrees, reporting that this now equates to twenty per cent of all pupils throughout the UK, That's a frightening one in five of all school aged children. The highest number ever recorded.

The recent YouGov commissioned survey, also found that eighty percent of teachers surveyed think children in their classroom are behind with their talking and/or understanding of words and seventy-three per cent of teachers surveyed think that

Children have Changed

children's speech and language is not prioritised by the Government. Perhaps even more worryingly, fifty-three per cent of teachers surveyed don't believe they have sufficient training to support pupils' speech and language in the classroom. Unfortunately, we also know the lifelong impact that unaddressed speech and language needs can have on a child:

- o They are six times more likely to be behind in English at age eleven.

- o Eleven times more likely to be behind in Maths at age eleven.

- o Twice as likely to develop a mental health condition

- o Twice as likely to be unemployed as an adult

It's well documented that at least sixty percent of young offenders have an unaddressed speech, language or communication delay. There's no getting away from it; we need to get better at recognising SLC delay and addressing it early. Children's life chances are at stake here.

Considerations for post Pandemic babies

Even before the pandemic the UK education system had difficulties identifying and helping children who were struggling with talking and understanding the meaning of words but since the COVID-19

Children have Changed

lockdowns, the problem hasn't just exacerbated. It's exploded!

Our children are up against it. Not least, because in addition to a steep rise in children experiencing significant delay in this area, there is a national shortage of speech therapists in the UK. On average, there is a twenty per cent deficit in the profession, UK wide. I've certainly experienced first-hand, families on extremely long waiting lists for therapy, meaning early intervention no longer happens early enough. The result is more children are struggling and are experiencing frustration.

Over the pandemic, children and families referred for therapy were assessed through a phone call at best, and at worst, not at all. This was of course the guidance at the time and was based on robust risk assessments to keep us safe. Face to face interactions were not allowed. Speech and Language therapists are not to blame for this, but we cannot and should not ignore the impact. The backlog of referrals is impacting on children born well after lockdowns had finished and it will continue to impact unless it is addressed. These gaps in early support programmes will shape our children's futures.

Masks

Babies and children watch their parent's face for cues as they are developing their speech, language and

Children have Changed

communication skills. They watch the shapes their parents' mouth forms to make words and they hear the corresponding sounds. Although none of us wore masks in our own homes, it's impossible to quantify how many opportunities to learn about speech production and sounds were missed due to masks covering our mouths and muffling our speech, especially when children were out and about. Think how many times people stop, smile and talk to a young baby in the street or the supermarket queue. How many interactions were lost because of the two-metre distance rule and face coverings? Small studies have been made around this, but there is no concrete evidence.

However, studies have proved that masks did have a significant effect on the children's emotion recognition accuracy. In other words, because of adults wearing masks, young children found it much more difficult to read expressions, especially happy and sad facial expressions. There are many implications here.

Children automatically respond to positive praise but if they couldn't read happy expressions, they may not have made this connection. Children in my experience, almost always respond to sadness with kindness, but if they couldn't read sad expressions, has that impacted on their ability to empathise? The honest answer is we simply don't know for sure, but the rising rates of SLC delay indicate that for our children's sake, we need to stay curious. Young children need plenty of time to

Children have Changed

catch up as the effects of face masks and social distancing continue to be evaluated.

Case study: Ezra's story

Ezra, a small boy with huge blue eyes, attends a lovely, welcoming childcare setting. When I first met him, he had just turned three, but he still wasn't using any clear words. Sadly, in the current context, that's not unusual any more. After the pandemic, lots of children aren't using clear words and as services are stretched thinly in our county, they will remain on waiting lists for some time before it's addressed. I'd come to see Ezra because as well as not having any clear speech, he wasn't making any attempt to communicate either.

Ezra struggles to maintain eye contact, even with familiar adults. He never approaches adults or children, even when he needs something. I sat near him for a while, letting him get used to an unfamiliar adult in his space. He didn't appear to register that I was near. I heard him making some soft noises to himself. These were not words, but repetitive sounds. I copied them exactly and Ezra looked in my direction, fleetingly. I smiled at him but he didn't respond.

A little later, when Ezra was transfixed on posting objects into a box, I joined him again and copied his play. Every time he posted a block, I posted one too. I tried to mirror his body language to reflect his

Children have Changed

movements exactly. He looked at me and this time, his eye contact was quite direct. I even got a fleeting smile.

Mirroring a child's play is often successful in finding a way in with children who struggle to communicate as it gives validation to their sounds and movements. At that point, two little boys came along to join us and jostled Ezra for the blocks. It was too much for him and he moved away. I followed him to a table of jigsaws. He didn't attempt to complete the jigsaws. Instead, he posted the pieces down a gap behind a cupboard.

"Ah ha!" I said to the supervisor. "He's interested in the posting schema."

"Yes," she agreed, "His play skills are quite delayed. He loves posting."

The supervisor called everyone to the carpet area for a story. Ezra didn't respond. He carried on posting jigsaw pieces. When his name was called, he didn't look towards the adult. I made some notes and stood back to watch the other children as the staff herded them to the carpet to sit down. A little girl stopped rolling the play dough into sausages and came to sit next to me.

"Hello," I said. "Have you had fun?"

She smiled and gave a little shrug.

Children have Changed

"Does she have any speech?" I ask the supervisor, discreetly.

"She did," she says, "but as the other children don't speak yet, we think she might have given up."

"How many of your children can speak clearly?"

"She was the only one."

I left the setting honestly not knowing who to be most concerned about.

The poverty gap.

The case study above, although extreme, is completely true. Evidence shows that there has been a disproportionate impact on children's speech and language if they are from disadvantaged backgrounds, but unless we start to address this in a more urgent way, it will continue to impact on children who aren't delayed. They will have fewer role models, less challenge, and are at risk of regressing.

According to The Royal College of Speech and Language Therapists, children living in poverty are fifty per cent more likely to start school with a delay in their speech language and communication. In some areas of deprivation, more than fifty per cent of children start school with delay in this area. There is a long way to go to reduce inequality. (Source DFE - Oct 2020 - Best practice in SLC.)

Children have Changed

Measures to support declining levels of SLC.

Before 2020, declining levels of Speech, Language and Communication were severe enough for UK Governments to introduce specific programmes to help mitigate this delay. In England the Department for Education published Best Start in Speech, Language and Communication in October 2020 and The Scottish Government's 2024 project also aims to support children's early speech and language development and reduce the equity gap in this area.

The Welsh Government had already started the Talk With Me programme as they were so concerned about plummeting literacy levels and poor PISA results. This has recently resulted in a brilliant suite of useful online resources for parents and practitioners which you can access by following the link below:

https://www.gov.wales/talk-with-me

How to Support Early Language Development

Babies and toddlers learn to speak through watching and listening to others. Their first role models are their family and then their child care providers. They gradually learn through these interactions that communication is valuable and enjoyable.

Children have Changed

We adapt our communication with babies, often without even thinking about it. We simplify our language, we use more repetition, and we speak softly with lots of expression and exaggeration. This simple form of language that parents often use when talking to their babies has its own term - Motherese.

Most people slip into these language patterns quite naturally when presented with a baby, and it's worth remembering, because for children who have delayed language development, and who are operating around the same age as babies, we can use this style of communication to support their development. This is not being patronising. Children need us to adapt the way we speak. As long as we are aware of the context and adapt what we say, it's supporting the child at the level they need.

Much of what babies and toddlers learn is non-verbal at first. They may see you grab a towel before every bath time and gradually start to realise that that object signals its bath time. Using the word towel and bath repetitively will gradually help them to understand that these sounds and objects are in some way related. They may watch you put your coat on and begin to notice that signal means it's time to go outside. If they hear the word out or outside at the same time, they will start to make the association.

Here are a few common associations:

- o   Towel and shampoo mean bath time

Children have Changed

- o Cup / bowl means dinner time

- o Pyjamas means bedtime

- o Wellies and coat mean outdoor time.

- o Car keys mean time to get in the car.

General advice for children with speech and language delay

Children experiencing a delay in their development need adults to:

- o Speak at a slower pace than normal

- o Leave plenty of time for a child to answer (often much, much longer than we realise)

- o Leave plenty of pauses to allow children to process language.

- o Break down instructions into one step at a time.

- o Keep your vocabulary as simple as possible.

- o Use something visual, like an object or a sign, to help them make the association with the word.

Children have Changed

The importance of visuals.

Visuals can be real objects, photographs, pictures, symbols, cards or signs. For children who haven't learned to talk yet, speaking to them in full sentences can be overwhelming if they haven't got the skills to process sentences. Consequently, they get lost. They suffer information overload and end up processing nothing. If you are using something visual to help them understand, it's still important to remember to say the spoken word alongside it so that children can make the association.

Good reasons to use visuals:

- o Visuals don't disappear. Words, once spoken, disappear into the ether. Visuals are permanent, concrete reminders.

- o They allow children time to process language.

- o Visuals can be quickly recognised and provide information without a child having to 'read 'them.

- o Visuals don't have an attitude (like sometimes speech can). They just are.

- o Visuals can support children to transition between activities or areas.

228

Children have Changed

- They help children to develop independence as once they understand them, children can start to use them themselves to communicate.

- For all of the above reasons, they help to reduce children's anxiety.

Suggestions for Childcare and Education settings to support language development.

- Make sure you are consistently using visual cues as part of your daily routine.

- A simple visual timetable of the key points in your day will support all children, not just those with delayed development. Knowing what is going to happen next reduces everyone's anxiety (even the staff).

- Make sure everyone working with your children has at least a basic level of training in speech language and communication. The *Talk with Me* resources on the Welsh Government website are a great place to start if you need training and advice on this.

- You don't have to be trained in sign language programmes or communication aids to use gestures and signs effectively. Choose a few signs or gestures that you can use throughout your routine and start using them today.

Children have Changed

o Do you ever provide children with a silent time? This need only be a few minutes, where they perhaps lie under a tree, or wrap themselves in a blanket and just listen. Stillness and silence are so precious in our busy lives and most children don't get enough of them.

o Think about the levels of background noise and distraction in your setting. Can you make sure there is no background noise when you are singing together or reading the children a story? Many children have little, if any time without background distractions today. Silence makes a difference to the way we process language.

o Allow yourselves regular time to reflect on how you support children's language development. There is a lot to remember and get right, but it's worth making the extra effort because when children start to talk, so many other obstacles fall away.

Children have Changed

Case study

I first met Conner and his Mum Chloe on a home visit. Conner had been referred to us by his health visitor when he'd failed to meet his expected milestones at his two-year check-up. I'm used to visiting homes where the main focus of the living room is a large TV, but I wasn't prepared for the immense, colossal, cinema sized, surround sound screen that dwarfed the tiny living room. It must have been draining the national grid. You could probably see it from space.

I squeezed myself into a corner, pulled out my trusty bag of assessment toys and sat on the floor with Conner.

"Could you turn the TV off please?" I practically shouted over the volume.

"He likes it," Chloe's arms folded defensively.

"Just for a moment please? I can't compete with cartoons."

"He'll scream if I turn it off."

"I'll try and distract him" I said, "I promise."

"But he'll fight me for the remote as soon as it goes off."

Children have Changed

"Can you put it somewhere out of sight for a bit then please?

Chloe reluctantly turned it off, "Sorry babe. Mums got to do it for a minute."
But Conner was already diving into my bag and showing an interest in some the sensory toys I'd brought.

As I sat and played with Conner, I managed to hold his attention quite nicely, but I noticed that it was Chloe that went and retrieved the remote, her finger hovering over it. I think she found the background silence troubling. While the TV was off, she constantly looked at her phone.

This was a visit with a lot to unpick.

The space and silence to hear language.

Conner hadn't picked up any words except some phrases he'd copied from a favourite programme, so Chloe was under the mistaken impression that having the TV on constantly was actually teaching Conner to learn to talk, rather than delaying his language.

With the health visitor's help, we gradually helped Chloe to understand that if the TV was on in the background all day, Conner's brain wasn't getting any space to process new language. There was simply no room for him to be able to hear new words and make connections without other signals from the screen

232

Children have Changed

hijacking them. Connor was having way over the NHS guidelines for screen time and it was impacting on his communication skills, speech, social communication, sleeping patterns and his emotional regulation.

The only language patterns he had managed to retain were *I'll do it* and *Oh No,* which were two phrases from a programme that he'd watched on repeat since he was a baby. But Conner wasn't using these phrases in context to communicate. He was repeating them parrot fashion. He needed plenty of opportunities to hear real language in context, without an onslaught of background sounds. His aggression and short attention span were a direct result of this screen overstimulation.

And yet, when I sat and played with Conner, he was able to give me a little attention. When given plenty of time he could follow a simple instruction and when I used a lot of repetition, he copied me and said the word pop, several times when we were blowing bubbles together. Chloe was amazed.

I almost always have to ask parents to turn off the TV when I go on a home visit. Most parents are flabbergasted when I tell them about the impact that screens can have on their child's language development. Modern society is setting some of our youngest children up to fail. There is no education programme for parents about this at any point before children enter school. At no point, either ani-natal or post-natal are the dangers of screen time are questioned or addressed with new parents.

Children have Changed

Tips for parents.

- Turn off the screen and talk to your child. You are infinitely better than a screen and your child *wants* your attention.

- Look at real books rather than stories on iPad's wherever you can. Visit the library and borrow books with plenty of entertainment value like pop-up and lift the flap books. Your child will benefit from hearing your voice, and you can't get social communication skills from an automated screen.

- Play alongside your child and mirror their vocalisations and actions as closely as you can. This allows a child to feel that their play is valuable and worthy of your attention and it can open up early channels of social communication.

- Play games together where you can introduce your child to simple turn taking activities, like passing a ball back and forth or taking turns to use a marble run. Learning to take turns lays the foundations for sharing with others.

- If you are worried about your child's speech, language, communication or their social communication skills always seek help from medical professionals.

Children have Changed

Conclusion

Children have Changed

Children have Changed

"What is happening to our young people? They disrespect their elders; they disobey their parents. They ignore the law. They riot in the streets, inflamed with wild notions. Their morals are decaying."

If that quote has a ring of familiarity and sounds like something your grandparents might say, you might be surprised to find that it was made in the fourth century BC, by Plato.

Since the beginning of time, there is evidence that parents and teachers worried about the next generation of children and how society will turn out once they come of age. It's a natural reaction to progression and change, but as I sit down to write this conclusion, I've just seen yet another headline stating that in a nearby region, there has been a sixty percent increase in the number of children identified to have special educational needs this year and I can't help reflecting:

- o How many of those children haven't had the right opportunities and experiences to be able to develop in line with their peer group?

- o How many of those children have missed out on playful, physical experiences and consequently have gaps in their development?

Children have Changed

- How many of those children have experienced early trauma, like domestic violence or are living with family members with significant mental health conditions?

- How many of those children have been pacified with screens and comfort food?

- How many of those children's parents haven't had early access to early health support programmes to help them with feeding, toileting, or sleep patterns.

- How many of these children if given access to an emotionally available adult, the right environment and plenty of time, would catch up?

- How many children will feel like a fish out of water when they go to school today?

- What will our society look like when these children come of age and leave school?

I work with young children who are experiencing significant developmental delay. Every day, I meet the most giving, loving parents who are often exhausted, worn down and at a loss, as they wait for health appointments and education placements to materialise.

I meet early years practitioners whose dedication means they are pulling out all the stops to provide

Children have Changed

environments where young children can play and learn at the appropriate stage for their development.

I meet caring, knowledgeable health professionals who are just as frustrated at the length of their waiting lists as parents are.

I meet teachers and headteachers who don't want to exclude young children because that goes against everything they stand for, but who feel they are left with no option when the behaviours that children arrive with just aren't acceptable in the school system we currently provide.

The role of health and social care.

Do you remember how, during the pandemic, hospitals were closed to all but the most serious life-threatening cases? NHS staff were overwhelmed with Covid 19 cases and staff were transferred from their usual roles to help deal with pandemic cases. As a result, outpatient appointments were cancelled or postponed. Where consultations did happen, they were made over the phone. Health visitors postponed home visits, resulting in many children not receiving timely support.

Early intervention works - we all know this. It's been proven. Keeping safe from a life-threatening virus had of course, to take priority, but the result of withdrawing or postponing early support and

239

Children have Changed

interventions is all too evident in many of our current early years children.

Equally, during the same time, many social care incidents were not addressed as early as they would usually have been, due to home visits being prioritised for only the most significant cases. Domestic violence figures rose during the pandemic, parent mental health conditions rose and many of those cases are only now coming to light.

Educational Psychology

Educational psychologists are invaluable in helping us to understand the child's perspective, and to guide us in providing the right support for individual children, but research published this summer by the Department for Education (DfE) found that 88% of councils were struggling to recruit EPs, while a third were struggling to retain them.

Recruitment in childcare.

Thousands of extra nursery workers and childminders are needed in the UK, as the expansion of funded hours is rolled out. By September 2025, all eligible pre-school children of working parents, from the age of nine months, will be able to access 30 hours of childcare during term time in England, but this offer comes at a time when childcare providers are leaving in droves. About 27,500 early-years professionals will be needed to meet the expected rise in demand for

Children have Changed

places, an estimated eight percent expansion of the current workforce, according to the think tank Nesta.

Working with early years children is physically and mentally demanding. I speak from experience. As well as needing eyes in the back of your head, there is lots of paperwork to complete, long hours and for many in the profession, they only receive the minimum wage. It is also one of the most important, rewarding, satisfying, *brilliant* jobs you can possibly do.

Neurological or Traumatic delay?

Sadly, without clear health evidence, we simply don't know if some of today's young children have a genuine neurological condition, or if they have been exposed to early traumatic experiences. Both can present with almost identical symptoms such as:

- o Reduced eye contact
- o Limited speech
- o Lack of social communication skills
- o Reduced interactions with adults and children
- o Stimming or repetitive behaviours to soothe themselves
- o Seeking intensive sensory input
- o Delay in toileting skills
- o Issues around food
- o Sleep disruption
- o Delay in play skills
- o Aggressive behaviours
- o Inappropriate emotional outbursts

Children have Changed

All of the above could be symptoms of adverse traumatic childhood experiences, but equally, could be early signs of a neurological condition and so health appointments are needed to explore the cause of these behaviours so that education can provide the most appropriate support.

In some cases, where a therapeutic approach has been consistently used, diagnosis of neurological conditions have actually been overturned, so it is really important that we stay open minded and curious. We need to get to know our children and their families so that we have the most holistic picture of a child that we can. In the meantime, putting diagnosis to one side, meeting each individual child where they are in their development, taking the time to play alongside them, and considering the reasons for their behaviour is the kindest and most positive way forward.

Last word.

Children have changed. I see it every day and I'm sure you do too. They are up against it in our current society. I sincerely hope the information and suggestions in this book have helped you at least begin to understand why children's behaviour is changing.

I hope it challenges you to think about why our current provision isn't always working for many of our young children who are experiencing delay. Getting rid of old systems can feel uncomfortable and

Children have Changed

disorientating and takes courage. But if *we* don't change, how will these children's needs be met?

As Dr. Maya Angelou says,

"Do the best you can until you know better, then when you know better, do better."

I'd add to that,

"...and as you are doing it, above all else, keep your sense of humour!"

Children have Changed

To find out more go to:

Estherevansauthor.co.uk

Children have Changed

Thank you to everyone working in Early Years – you are the most amazing people.
Thanks to Paula and Terri for the teamwork.
Thank you to Shrewsbury and Oswestry writers for all the positive comments and the motivation to keep writing, especially Sally, Jenny, Jan, Jorge, Liz and Megan.
Thank you to Ruby, Lydia and Gracie for the feedback, suggestions and all the happy memories and most of all, thank you to Jason.

Children have Changed

Printed in Great Britain
by Amazon